ABOUT THE AUTHOR

Anthony Stevens has a B.A. from Cambridge University, an M.A. from McMaster University and a Ph.D. from Leicester University, all in English Literature. He has taught many different aspects and periods of drama and theatre in schools and universities, and he has written, devised and directed many plays. Currently he teaches International Baccalaureate English A1, Theatre Arts and Theory of Knowledge in a private school in Greece and Attic Tragedy in the College Year in Athens program.

How Plays Tell Stories

Studying Drama as Literature

Anthony Stevens

Anagnosis
Athens, Greece

Anagnosis
Deliyianni 3
151 22 Maroussi
Athens, Greece
www.anagnosis.gr

ISBN 960-88087-6-6

© Anthony Stevens 2006

All rights reserved.
No part of this book may be reproduced,
stored in a retrieval system,
or transmitted in any form or by any means,
without the prior permission in writing of the author.
The customary exceptions are recognised for the purpose of
research, private study, criticism, or review.

Photoset and printed by:
K. Pletsas - Z. Karadri O.E.
Harilaou Trikoupi 107
Athens
www.typografio.gr

PREFACE

Studying drama differs in certain significant ways from studying poetry or narrative fiction or prose non-fiction. Arguably, drama is a relatively difficult genre to appreciate. This is because drama is not written to be read by readers at home or on planes or trains, but to be performed in the theatre. It is primarily written, thus, for actors, directors and designers. This is not to say that plays should not be counted as 'literature' after all. It is to say, however, that the proper appreciation of plays as literature requires an understanding of the way they have been written with the goal of performance in mind.

This book has been written as a guide to all relevant aspects of the study of drama for the International Baccalaureate Language A1. However, it will serve as a guide to the study of plays in any literature course at pre-undergraduate level or at first-year undergraduate level. Its principal goal is to help the student see the play text in relation to all the various considerations and choices that the experienced, professional dramatist has in mind in writing plays for the stage rather than for the page. It should also be found useful by those teachers who are have studied literature but have little experience of the theatre and hence feel less confident about teaching drama.

As a course in literature, Language A1 has two main functions. One is to provide a suitable foundation and qualification for the study of literature at undergraduate level for students with this ambition. The other is to promote an appreciation of literature and of the cultures of which it is a vital part among future engineers, lawyers, doctors, and so on. Hence all International Baccalaureate Diploma students must take a Language A1 course. In this course, they study not only the literature of their own language and culture but also, through the World Literature component, that of other languages and cultures.

The current Language A1 syllabus is organized in large part around the concept of *genre*. At Higher Level, students must study at least four different genres; at Standard Level, they must study at least three. For very many languages, drama is included as a genre. The majority of Langage A1 students around the world, in fact, are likely to study some drama as part of their course. Some students will study a great deal of drama.

The Language A1 syllabus allows the teacher great scope in the choice of texts. This book therefore ranges widely in its examples, which are almost all taken from the list of Prescribed World Literature texts and from the English A1 Prescribed Book List (which lists playwrights rather than named plays). In relation to the former, an important aim of the book is to promote some understanding of the variation in the concept and practice of drama from culture to culture. Moreover, plays by Shakespeare figure largely among the examples both because of their importance in world drama and because English A1 students must study at least one Shakespeare play. However, no specific example is treated in extensive detail, for two reasons. Firstly, the range of choice teachers have means that actual 'set texts' cannot be easily predicted. Secondly, and much more importantly, it is up to the student herself or himself to carry out the detailed analysis of specific plays, either alone or together with other students and a teacher. This book aims to provide the conceptual tools to make that possible, not to do it on the student's behalf.

One other point about the use of examples is worth making here. To the extent that we can identify general rules about the nature of plays, then specific examples serve to illustrate these rules. But the most general rule of drama, as of all the arts, is that 'all rules have exceptions'. Examples of such exceptions have special significance, for they should guide the student to apply the rules flexibly and with caution.

Following the Introduction, the first four chapters develop the main conceptual framework necessary for a properly focused study of drama. Together, they provide a guide to how plays work. Chapter One covers the different ways in which plays can be considered as 'dramas' or as being 'dramatic' and the various implications of these terms. Chapter Two explores how characters in plays are constructed and how they function. Chapter Three deals with the ways in which the action of plays is organized in order to achieve dramatic unity or 'wholeness,' or certain effects upon the audience. Lastly, Chapter Four examines how playwrights writing for the theatre can make use of a wide range of 'theatrical effects' as means to achieve their intentions. Each of these four chapters ends with a set of questions that students should ask of their set plays. These questions serve as a kind of summary of the key ideas and concepts of the chapter.

Literature of all genres is most effectively studied when the student tries – and manages – to 'put himself or herself in the dramatist's or novelist's or poet's shoes'. The first, second and fourth chapters of **How Plays Tell Stories** therefore include a number of specially devised *writing exercises* which isolate particular features of the craft of writing for the theatre and challenge the student to solve certain problems of dramatization. In actually tackling them, the student will gain a much more intimate knowledge of how dramatic writing works, although simply thinking about them will also have benefit.

Next, Chapter Five broadens the perspective by exploring how the study of drama relates to Theory of Knowledge. It tries to answer the following questions: what exactly is *knowledge of* drama and can we acquire knowledge of other things *through drama*? These questions would be worth tackling independently of the needs of a Theory of Knowledge course. To answer them adequately is to understand why drama matters.

The broad range of theatre is expressed in the common image of two masks, one laughing, the other grieving, which represent tragedy and comedy. Although not all plays fit into one or other category, or into the related category of tragicomedy, students studying plays of these types will benefit from an overview of their main features. This is provided in the Appendix.

Lastly, an index of dramatists and plays referred to is provided for easy reference, as well as an extensive glossary of the most important drama-related terms.

CONTENTS

Preface 5

Introduction: Reading 'Dramatic Literature' 9

Chapter One: What exactly is 'drama'? 19
Chapter Two: The 'Persons of the Drama' 35
Chapter Three: Dramatic Structure 51
Chapter Four: Theatrical Means and Ends 71
Chapter Five: Drama and Theory of Knowledge 89

Appendix: Tragedy, Comedy and Tragicomedy 101

Glossary of drama-related terms 113

Index of playwrights and plays 123

THE *WRONG* APPROACH

THE COUNT: What is your opinion of the play?

BANNAL (*a critic*): Well, who's it by?

THE COUNT: That is a secret for the present.

BANNAL: You don't expect me to know what to say about a play when I don't know who the author is, do you?

THE COUNT: Why not?

BANNAL: Why not! Why not!! Suppose you had to write about a play by Pinero and one by Jones! Would you say exactly the same thing about them?

THE COUNT: I presume not.

BANNAL: Then how could you write about them until you knew which was Pinero and which was Jones? Besides, what sort of play is this? That's what I want to know. Is it a comedy or a tragedy? Is it a farce or a melodrama? Is it repertory theatre tosh, or really straight paying stuff?

GUNN: Can't you tell from seeing it?

BANNAL: I can see it all right enough; but how am I to know how to take it? Is it serious, or is it spoof? If the author knows what his play is, let him tell us what it is. If he doesn't, he can't complain if I don't know either. *I'm* not the author.

THE COUNT: But is it a good play, Mr Bannal? That's a simple question.

BANNAL: Simple enough when you know. If it's by a good author, it's a good play, naturally. That stands to reason. Who is the author? Tell me that; and I'll place the play for you to a hair's breadth.

From *FANNY'S FIRST PLAY* (1911),
by GEORGE BERNARD SHAW

INTRODUCTION
READING 'DRAMATIC LITERATURE'

Plays are written to be performed.

For this reason, it is sometimes argued that drama should not be treated as a form of 'literature,' in other words that plays should not be seen as texts that can be fully understood and appreciated simply by means of reading (together, perhaps, with some follow-up discussion). Play texts, in this view, can only be truly understood in the full context of the art of theatre, in relation to the complex process by which they come to be turned into the 'real thing' – the play in performance.

For a Theatre Arts or Performing Arts course, this point of view is perfectly valid. But it is also a little misleading.

While it is true that a play fully exists, or 'comes to life,' only in performance, it is also true that a play is not the same thing as any particular performance or any particular production of it. However interesting and artistically worthwhile a particular production may be, the play, in the form of a text, continues to exist as a potentiality for further, different productions. In one sense, then, a play text is *less* than any performance of it, for as a text it does not contain all those things that actors and designers can bring to it in the way of intonation, gesture, costume, set and so on. But in another sense it is *more* than any specific performance, for it contains the possibility of other, different performances. At least this is so if it can be described as a *good* play.

Moreover, play texts survive, whereas play productions do not (although since the invention of film and video this is not quite so true as it was). Theatre is an ephemeral art, hence much of what we know of its history rests on surviving play texts. More importantly still, theatre history becomes a *living tradition* almost entirely because of the survival of texts, for old plays are available for performance today. Even if they are not performed as they originally would have been, their differences from modern plays (differences which are evident in the texts) make new and sometimes strange demands on actors, directors and designers and thus enrich the theatre of today. But here too we are led to the same point: old plays are worth reviving only if they are *good*.

In this book we will be concerned to understand what qualities make a good play, as distinct from a good production or a good performance, and how these qualities can be discovered by reading.

What can be called *text-based theatre* (theatre where production starts from an already existing script) is not the only kind of theatre, of course. Some productions are *devised*. In the latter case some actors, together, perhaps, with others, invent characters, situations and plots through workshop improvisations, either based on some kind of research or simply by using their imaginations.

It is sometimes suggested that text-based theatre places the actors, designers and director in the position of *interpreters*, whose role is to interpret the script and hence the intentions of the playwright, while in devised work the actors are themselves the *creators*. This is one reason why some theatre workers have a kind of prejudice against or at least a suspicion of the text; they prefer the latter role to the former, not necessarily because it has 'higher status' but because it seems to offer more freedom. However, this distinction is over-simplified. A good play text engages the creativity of actors and others. It should challenge them to find the most creative solutions to the problems it poses. In any case, interpretation of this kind – artistic interpretation – is surely creative in itself, unlike critical interpretation.

Even so, it is interesting that text-based productions tend to have a different 'feel' than devised productions. As a rough generalization, devised work is often more actor-centred and theatrically playful while text-based work is often more character-centred and dramatically compressed.

Text-based theatre itself is not uniform in its practice, for in the production process the text can be approached in different ways – ways which give the text greater or lesser authority.

We can provisionally distinguish between two different approaches to the staging of play texts. One begins by asking '*How can this play be done?*' while the other begins by asking '*What can be done with this play?*' The former is concerned to discover what is actually in the play and to bring this out in performance. The latter brings the 'director's vision' to it and even imposes that vision upon it. In the latter case the text is seen not so much as something to be explored but as a starting point or 'springboard' for something else.

Still, while this distinction is useful, it seems more straightforward than it really is. The reason is that *any* text-based production necessarily both *finds things in* the play as a text and *brings things to* it. One approach puts more emphasis on 'finding things' while the other puts more emphasis on 'bringing things'. In practice, however, it is not always possible to tell the difference!

It seems reasonable to say that a good play 'has more in it' than a poor play. Hence there is more for a production to discover and to bring out in performance. However, what we consider to be good plays are often those which are most open to different theatrical interpretation. Shakespeare's *Hamlet*, for example, is considered great not just because of the profundity of its themes and the richness of its dramatic language, but also because there are endless ways in which the lead role can be played. Of course, this does not mean that *any* way of acting the part of Hamlet is valid. What it does suggest is that what is 'in' the text of a good play is complex, more a set of possibilities than a single, simple actuality. And this implies that what is 'in' the play as a text is like an invitation to bring something to it, so that the difference between these things is like that between two sides of a coin.

The student who has to study plays as part of a literature course should adopt an attitude towards the text which is like that of the director who asks 'How can this play be done?' However, s/he must keep in mind that a play text does not usually provide precise and simple answers to all the questions it raises about how it 'should' be performed.

WRITING AND THE ORIGINS OF THEATRE

It is commonly said that theatre began in ancient Athens at the end of the sixth century BCE. This claim is sometimes criticized as 'Eurocentric,' but if there is a prejudice behind it, it is a prejudice of a different kind.

Sometimes it is asserted that the rituals of various other cultures are performances and even that they have 'theatrical' qualities. But it is surely a mistake to confuse ritual performance with theatrical performance. In the latter, there is a consciousness of *pretence* in both performers and audience alike, but in the former, neither participants nor congregation think of what is being 'performed' as involving pretence. In spite of this, however, it is the case that some kinds of *dramatic enactment* occur in different cultures as component parts of certain rituals and ceremonies. That is, certain acts that are acknowledged as pretence can occur within the larger context of something which is not pretence. These tend to be small-scale and undeveloped. Even so, it is possible to apply this model to Greece too; after all, plays were performed there as part of a festival in honour of the god Dionysos.

But this still misses the key point. The plays produced in Greece were first *written*. This had two profound consequences. Firstly, it allowed dramatic fictions to be constructed which were both more complex and more tightly organized than would have been possible without the means of writing. Secondly, it allowed the playwrights to vary and adapt the existing stories in original ways, since there was no threat that any version would be lost from memory. To refer to this as '*the* origin of theatre' may be to express a bias for literate culture over oral culture, but it remains true that much of the history of theatre as we know it was made possible by writing.

We should also acknowledge here that theatre in a developed and sophisticated form emerged in India too, almost certainly before Alexander the Great brought any Hellenistic influence to the region. We know less about how and exactly when this happened than we do about the Greek theatre, but the existence of writing was clearly a precondition in India too. However, the Indians did not follow the Greeks, or rather Aristotle, in emphasizing the importance of the literate aspects of theatre over its other aspects, but continued to place equal value on music, movement and gesture in performance, in their theoretical writings as well as in their practice.

Since plays are written to be performed they are not written *for readers* in the same sense that novels and poems are written for readers. Nonetheless they are available for reading in printed form and it is self-evident that the director and actors must read the text as a necessary part, if only a relatively small part, of the passage from page to stage.

It is also the case that plays share some things with other literary genres. They tell (usually fictional) stories, involving characters in settings; they may use heightened or figurative language to do so, including 'literary devices' such as imagery and parallelism; and so on. It seems reasonable to ask, then, whether – within the context of a course in literature – plays can be read as if they were a kind of 'abridged novels' – novels with all the narrative parts left out. This might not be the best way to study them, but might it yet be 'good enough'?

To answer this, let's first take a step back, to ask what the study of literature really is. We can begin by translating the phrase as the *study of verbal art*. To study such a thing, the key is for the student to put herself or himself *in the position of the writer*, for understanding an art is not the same thing as simply being moved or affected by it. Understanding an art is effectively understanding the kinds of choices that an artist has and the reasons (conscious or unconscious) for making particular choices.

Now, a playwright writes plays that are intended for performance, not 'abridged novels'. Hence to read and study plays as if they were abridged novels is most definitely not to put oneself in the position of the writer. This can only lead to misunderstanding, not to understanding. Although the student of literature is not involved in any process of staging the play, in order to see things from the playwright's point of view s/he must read it as written for just such a process.

The hostility to treating drama as literature noted at the beginning of this Introduction is in fact most valid when it is a hostility to the idea and practice of reading plays as if they were unproblematically like novels or poems. But once we learn how to read plays for what they really are, it becomes perfectly legitimate – and rewarding – to study them as part of a literature course. The following chapters are intended to help students to read plays 'for what they really are'. This does not mean studying the technicalities of the production and rehearsal process but coming to understand what it means for a writer to write with staging and performance in mind. This makes a lot of difference. As we shall see, even a basic concept like *character* needs to be thought of differently in relation to plays than in relation to novels and short stories.

THE 'READABILITY' OF PLAYS

Considered in general and not just in relation to play texts, it is important to note that there are different kinds of reading. Given any novel, poem or play text, we can distinguish between *what* it says and *how* it says it. It is possible to read the text for the 'what' (simply in order, that is, to understand its meaning) or for the 'how' (in order to grasp the way in which that meaning is produced). The latter is commonly called 'critical reading'.

A critical reading is similar to what is called a 'professional reading,' though these terms are not perfectly synonymous. The idea here is that the reader adopts the point of view of the producer of the text (who is commonly a professional) in order to see why it has been written as it has. In relation to drama, the term 'professional reading' may be preferable, if only to avoid thinking of plays as like novels or poems where 'critical reading' rules. (But note that an amateur can work in a wholly 'professional' way – as is often the case in theatre – in the sense that her or his skills and standards are high. A 'professional reading' is professional in the same sense.)

What, then, should we call the other kind of reading identified above, reading for the 'what' of a text, reading which simply focuses on identifying and grasping what the meaning is? Note that in the case of narrative fiction this kind of reading is usually *intended*; it is the kind of reading that the producer of a text expects its target-audience to perform. But it should not be called the 'intended reading,' at least it should not be called this in a fully general way, because it is not the way a play text is intended to be read. In fact, given that plays are intended for performance, the intended reading of a *play text* is a kind of professional reading. That is, directors, designers and actors read plays in relation to their own professional goals in staging the play, but in order to do so they need to understand the professional contribution already made by the writer in the form of a script.

The student of drama should aim to acquire and develop the ability to read texts 'professionally,' not exactly as actors, directors and designers read them, but by 'putting themselves in the playwright's shoes'. However, it is important that plays – or some plays – can also be read in a 'non-professional' way. At some points in the history of theatre, in fact, plays were written with this in mind. In ancient Rome, for example, Seneca's tragedies were written for private reading, not theatrical presentation. Nonetheless, they were written for *reading aloud*. In the late nineteenth century, the Norwegian dramatist Henrik Ibsen depended for his income on sales of his plays in book form; thus, although he wrote his plays for performance (and very skillfully), he also wrote them so that readers could readily imagine and follow the action on the page.

At least in the case of some plays, it is possible, even easy, to follow the story line and to come to a reasonably good understanding of the characters without needing to make any attempt to imagine how the play might be staged. Where this is the case, I shall call the play *readable* or say that it has high *readability*. But not all plays are 'readable' in this sense. More accurately, plays vary greatly in their degree of 'readability'.

In reading a play text, the reader usually encounters two distinct kinds of language. Apart from the names which identify the speaking characters, these kinds of language are *speech*, either dialogue or monologue, and *stage directions*. Now, it is a significant fact about written drama that, with few exceptions, the proportion of stage directions to speech is very low. In fact, the manuscripts of early plays usually had no stage directions at all. These were added by later editors for the (supposed) benefit of readers, sometimes superfluously and occasionally misleadingly. Stage directions became used more commonly in manuscripts as the style of speech became more 'naturalistic,' that is, more like the language of everyday life. Before this, the heightened, often poetic speech of plays was written so as to convey or suggest all necessary information concerning setting and action. In the interest of maintaining the 'naturalness' of speech, later playwrights began to shift some of this information into stage directions, but it is still striking that these remain rare compared to speech. Setting is typically given in a stage direction at the beginning of a play, or of one of its acts, but the writer of naturalistic drama still tries to *imply* as much of the action as possible by means of the dialogue.

Why should this be? As far as the main actions which make up the backbone of the play's plot are concerned, the dialogue will relate to these in one way or another, explicitly or implicitly, and thus they can be deduced from it. The dramatist will only need to specify an action in a stage direction if either its precise nature or its precise timing cannot be inferred in this way. As for the other kind of direction which indicates how a speech is to be spoken (for example, "*angrily*" or "*sotto voce*"), again this can often be deduced from the situation, or it is implied by the way the speech is worded, or it can be left to the creative judgment of the director and actor. Given this, a playwright who includes abundant stage directions is either a) a poor playwright, or b) lacking in confidence in the ability of directors and actors (which is one way of being a 'poor playwright'), or c) writing for a very different kind of theatre than that which is usually transmitted in script form, that is, for so-called 'physical theatre'. The only examples of the latter that a student of Language A1 is likely to come across are *Act Without Words I* and *Act Without Words II* by Samuel Beckett, each of which, as its title suggests, is the script of a pantomime consisting entirely of directions.

> Perhaps the most important rule for analyzing drama, or any art, is that 'all rules have exceptions'. Eugene O'Neill is not in the least a 'poor playwright,' yet his powerful drama *Long Day's Journey Into Night* includes a very high proportion of extraordinarily detailed stage directions. These either specify the precise appearance of the characters, down to the length of their fingers or the brightness of their eyes, or give elaborate instructions as to gesture, tone and attitude during many of the speeches. There seem to be two principal reasons for this. Firstly, the work is autobiographical. In order to 'confront his own demons,' O'Neill seems to have needed to imagine everything in the most vivid detail. Secondly, and more importantly, the play deals with a family in crisis, and powerful and dangerous tensions, all rooted in the past, underlie every action. These destructive *undercurrents* cannot be communicated in the dialogue alone. However, they can be grasped from the way the action unfolds, as they break through the surface, and to this extent a director and actors would be able to 'find them' retrospectively in the earlier dialogue too, in other words to use the knowledge gained later in the play to inform and shape its first stages during rehearsal. But for a reader, this is not the case. Directors and actors know that a reading is just a first step in a long process of discovery. A reader, however, tends to expect all or most to be clear from a single reading. O'Neill seems to have written 'unnecessarily many' stage directions with this kind of reader in mind.

Usually, plays with high 'readability' tend not to be any less 'readable' than they might have been had many more stage directions been used. If they are well written, then all the dialogue's implications for action will be as clear to a reader as to an actor. (But a play like *Long Day's Journey Into Night* would lose some of its 'readability' with fewer stage directions.)

There are two basic reasons why some plays lack or have relatively low 'readability' in the sense defined. The first is where the significance of the play in performance depends less on the dramatic interaction of characters and the unfolding of the plot or story line and more on what can provisionally be called its 'theatricality' (this term will be explained later in this Introduction). For most readers it is easier to imagine characters and events, by imagining these as they might appear in real life, than it is to imagine action on stage, particularly where the latter is stylized or highly theatrical or simply non-naturalistic.

The other kind of 'low readability' arises for a different reason, one which has to do with the very nature of dramatic dialogue. In many kinds of drama characters generally 'say what they mean and mean what they say,' but in some kinds of drama this is far from being true. In the latter case the significance of a play lies to a great extent in what is called its *subtext*. As this term implies, the real meaning of the action (including the characters' motives and goals) is not exactly 'in' the text but 'under' it. From a (non-professional) reader's point of view this reliance on subtext may give rise to a feeling that something dramatic is taking place but without it being fully clear what exactly this is, as in a play such as Pinter's *Old Times*, or it may give rise to the feeling that nothing very dramatic is taking place at all, as in Chekhov's *The Cherry Orchard*.

Play texts with 'high readability' are easier for the student to write about using an all-purpose vocabulary of literary criticism: plot, character, setting, style, motive, climax, denouement... and so on. Plays with low readability require a vocabulary which is more specific to drama and theatre, although some of the all-purpose terms will still apply. But the former type of plays will be better discussed and more fully understood if the latter vocabulary is available too.

> In what is often called 'the first work of literary criticism,' the *Poetics*, the Greek philosopher Aristotle asserts that "the tragic effect" is possible without a performance. In other words, the essential effect that a tragedy has upon the spectators in the theatre can also be experienced in reading the play. In Aristotle's view, the spectacle – which covers all visual aspects of the play in performance – is the "least artistic" part of a tragedy. There is clearly some 'literary bias' here, but this may be partly explained by the fact that the performances with which Aristotle was familiar were mounted during the fourth century BCE, well after the genre of Greek tragedy had gone into decline (the beginning of this decline being usually associated with the defeat of Athens in the Peloponnesian war in 404). Even so, Aristotle's point holds true for a good amount of serious drama, or tragedy, that which has what I have called 'high readability'. But as far as ancient Greek tragedy itself is concerned, one essential aspect of the plays which is difficult to access by reading and which certainly contributes to the tragic effect in its fullest sense is the role of the chorus, especially as it sang and danced.

THE *DRAMATIC* AND *THEATRICAL* ASPECTS OF PLAYS

An audience watching a play in a theatre is affected by many things. Some of these things contribute to an appreciation of the *play* itself. Some contribute to an appreciation of the *performance* or *production*. And some (such as a person constantly whispering in the row behind) contribute to neither, but rather detract from them. Obviously the third of these does not concern us here. Less obviously, nor does the second. In Hamlet's phrase, then, "The play's the thing".

It is important that we can distinguish between the play and the performance or production of it. Reading good play reviews helps clarify the distinction. A good review discusses, on the one hand, the merits of the play's plot, characterization, dialogue, and so on, as well as, on the other hand, the quality of individual performances, the appropriateness of the direction and design, and such like. Now, ordinary spectators make exactly the same basic distinction in their minds as they watch the play, although they may not be so skilled at *evaluating* the different elements of performance and production. But while the ordinary spectator may make some basic value judgments of the play itself (that it was 'boring' or 'gripping,' for example), s/he naturally has more of a predisposition to take the play *on its own terms* than does the professional critic. The ordinary spectator, that is, is more inclined to make a 'willing suspension of disbelief' and less inclined to ask whether the playwright's dialogue is terse or 'flabby' or whatever. We should respect this attitude. It is precisely the attitude that the playwright expects in his audience.

We are concerned here to distinguish the dramatic and theatrical aspects *of plays* – not of performances or productions. Drama is quite a slippery concept and will be dealt with at more length in Chapter One, but it seems clear that it is the play itself which seems to have drama or to be dramatic and not the way it is staged. Of course, the way the play is staged is intended to bring out the play's drama and some productions will bring it out more than others, but this does not alter the basic point. It is not so clear, however, that 'theatricality' is an aspect of the play itself rather than of its performance or production. It may not be. But if we are led to judge the performance or production as 'theatrical,' we probably mean that it is *too* theatrical for the play in question. Where this is not the case, where, that is, a 'theatrical' staging is appropriate for the play, then it is reasonable to think of the play itself as having a theatrical aspect.

Theatricality too is a difficult concept and will be discussed much more fully in Chapter Four. Here, we will simply make a basic and provisional distinction between the dramatic and theatrical aspects of plays. This distinction is of very great importance for the study of plays.

Whatever seems dramatic in a play is an aspect or quality of the play's fiction. The sense of drama arises in the fictional action presented onstage, in the interaction of the characters and in the unfolding of the plot. For this reason, if a film version of the play is made (not a filmed record of a theatre production, but an adaptation for the cinema), then, if this version is reasonably faithful to the original play, it will tend to be dramatic in much the same way as the play, in other words it will tend to communicate the 'same drama'.

Although for more than two thousand years the theatre – or rather live performance – was the only medium for drama, nowadays we are able to experience dramas in the cinema, on DVD and on television. This fact implies that drama is not intrinsically related to the means of theatrical production. Live theatre is now just one means of creating drama among others.

The very term 'theatricality,' on the other hand, implies that this, whatever it is, is intrinsic to theatre. We can define it like this: **whatever seems *theatrical* in a play is an aspect or quality of *certain ways in which the means of theatre are used to present the fiction.***

This needs clarifying. Firstly, the 'means of theatre' are the stage itself (or playing space), the actors, their costumes, the objects which make up the set, props (short for 'stage properties,' that is, certain objects that are used by the actors), lights, and such like. All these things are *real*. Moreover, an audience in the theatre actually sees these real things, at least most of them; in contrast, an audience in the cinema does not actually see the real things that were used in making the film, but only the filmed record or trace of them. At the same time, these real things are used to create a fiction: the stage is not just a stage, but a prison cell, or a battlefield; the set is not just two boxes but seats on a train, or a cliff looking out over the sea; the actor is not just an actor but a perplexed young man called Hamlet. Now, in some kinds of play the audience is implicitly invited to ignore the reality of the real thing and to focus entirely on the fictional identity given to it. But in other kinds of plays the attention of the audience is drawn to the *transformation* of the real thing into the fictional thing. Where this happens we can say that the effect is 'theatrical'. It is an effect which may contribute to the significance of the play and to its value as a work of theatrical art.

A straightforward example of this sense of theatricality is the use of mime. Suppose then that two actors, impersonating prisoners, have to mime the back-breaking work of shoveling piles of sand. Each shovels his own pile of sand into a (mimed) wheelbarrow which he pushes to the other's pile, emptying it there. In this way the sand is merely exchanged and the work can never be completed. A whistle blows. The men stand alongside each other and mime being handcuffed and shackled together. Then they are forced to run. Three-legged, they cannot run fast enough. They mime being beaten for this, still handcuffed and shackled together....

This is the opening of Athol Fugard's powerful play, *The Island*. (Strictly speaking, it is not 'Fugard's play' in the usual sense in which plays are attributed to authors. It was devised by Fugard together with the actors John Kani and Winston Ntshona.) If the scene were *not* mimed, the production would need real sand, real shovels, real wheelbarrows, real handcuffs and shackles, and a real third actor to carry out the beating. Without any of these, everything depends on the physical skills of the actors to make the audience 'see' them. Of course, the audience does not *literally* see these things; instead, it 'reads' the mime and imagines them. In so doing, the audience remains one hundred percent aware that what it is witnessing is a mime. That is, no 'illusion' is created. Thus, the audience 'sees' (imagines) the *characters* shoveling sand, etc., and simultaneously sees (literally) the *actors* performing the mime. This *double awareness* is an awareness of the real means of theatre, the actors themselves, being used – using themselves – to create a fictional scene, two prisoners forced to carry out hard labour and being otherwise abused in the notorious Robben Island prison during the Apartheid regime in South Africa.

This is a powerful theatrical effect, but how does it contribute to the significance of the play and to its value as a work of theatrical art? Note that such effects are often impressive – one admires the actors' skills – but they are only *significant* if they relate to the specific themes of the specific play. In this case, the effect is significant in several ways. Firstly, the intense physical work of hard labour is signified not simply by imitating it but also by *paralleling* or '*echoing*' it in the intense physical effort of the mime itself. Secondly, the two prisoners in this play are going to stage their own performance in prison of Sophocles' *Antigone*, a play about rebellion, something which, given their lack of resources, they can only do in a minimal and inventive way. The mime at the beginning of *The Island* serves to 'add value' to the idea of this kind of theatre, theatre which makes do with very little, increasing our respect for the literally 'amateur' but powerfully committed performance of the prisoners. Lastly, and more generally, mime is one common feature of what is called 'poor theatre' or 'rough theatre,' where these terms are not in the least negative. This is a kind of theatre which can express in its very theatricality the necessary inventiveness of an oppressed and impoverished group, as black South Africans were under Apartheid.

Theatricality takes many forms apart from mime, as will be explored more fully in Chapter Four. The important point here is that theatricality is not – or not necessarily – something which is *added* to a play text by actors and a director during the production process. Theatricality can be written into the play by the playwright and for this reason it is necessary for the student of plays, even the student of plays as 'dramatic literature,' to understand how it arises and above all how it can contribute to a play's significance and value.

CONVENTIONS

One of the most important concepts for the study of plays is that of *conventions*. Its sense is outlined here in the Introduction because of its importance, but large sections of most of the chapters that follows are discussions of different dramatic and theatrical conventions, whether or not the term is explicitly used within the discussion. Broadly, a convention is an accepted way of doing something. The unwritten rules which govern our social lives, such as shaking hands with certain people, using the right hand to do so, or using knives and forks to eat certain meals, are conventions. To say this is to say that there is nothing *necessary* about them. That is, any convention might have been different. But to say this, of course, is not to suggest that conventions can be broken with impunity.

In relation to plays, conventions are the 'rules' that apply to the representation of human life on stage during certain periods and for certain cultures or sub-cultures. Such conventions vary from period to period and from country to country. It was a convention of ancient Greek tragedy, for example, that violent acts were never represented as taking place on stage. In Elizabethan and Jacobean theatre, in contrast, violence is commonly represented, often graphically. Also in Elizabethan and Jacobean theatre, characters may speak *soliloquies* (monologues in which they 'think aloud' while alone) and *asides* (words which are presumed not to be heard by some or all of the other characters on stage). In the naturalistic theatre which emerged at the end of the nineteenth century, in contrast, soliloquies and asides are not permitted. The use of mime is a convention, since mime is appropriate for a certain set of plays but not for a different set, as is the use of verse, since some plays are written in heightened poetic language while others are written in everyday prose. In some plays a character may turn and directly address the audience, while other plays would be ruined if this were to occur.

Lastly, note that there are conventions of performance and staging too, independent of the conventions governing the play as a text. A convention of Shakespeare's theatre, for example, was that all parts were played by male actors, while a convention of ancient Greek tragedy as performed in Athens in the 5th century BCE was that the performers wore masks. We shall ignore these kinds of conventions as largely irrelevant to the study of plays as texts, although some would argue that the conventions of original production probably had some influence on the nature of the plays that were written at the time.

CHAPTER ONE
WHAT EXACTLY IS 'DRAMA'?

We use the noun 'drama' and the associated adjective 'dramatic' in a number of related but nonetheless distinct senses. There are three main senses.

Firstly, drama denotes a specific kind of *activity* which people engage in. This is the sense of the word when it appears in phrases like 'drama club' or 'drama class' or even 'drama therapy'. The activity of drama involves enactment and performance, though not necessarily directed towards the production of plays or public performance. In this activity, scenes and situations are acted out. Such scenes and situations are not necessarily fictional (they may be taken from the lives of the participants or from other documentary sources), and the characters involved or roles played are not necessarily invented (for the same reason), but they remain an 'imitation of life' rather than life itself in more or less the same way that children's games often imitate adult situations. Drama in this sense is often justified not in terms of its *product* – a polished or well-rehearsed performance – but in terms of the *process* through which the participants may discover things about themselves and even about actual real-life situations.

Secondly, drama denotes a specific kind of *form* in which a story can be presented or told. Note, however, that a phrase like 'the story is a drama' is ambiguous, for the third sense of drama (to be outlined below) may be implied. For this reason it is preferable to say 'the story is in dramatic form'. This means that the events which constitute the story, or more accurately the part of the story which is enacted in performance, are presented in the form of action rather than in the form of a report, for drama in this sense is implicitly distinguished from narrative. Note then that it is just as reasonable to say that a play text is in dramatic form as it is to say this of a play in performance, for dramatic form is recognizable on the page as well as on the stage or screen.

The third sense of drama is the most difficult to tie down. We can say that in this sense drama denotes a certain *quality* of the represented action, but it is not easy to go on to say exactly what this quality is. It is a quality which engages, involves and perhaps excites or moves a watching audience. This sense of the word is involved in the common distinction between (serious) drama and (non-serious) comedy. If a film is marketed as a drama you do not go to see it expecting to be made to laugh. (Note here, however, that comedy is often very serious. It can be serious in its subject matter, themes and in its 'message' – if it can be described as having one; but it does not present its own seriousness in a serious way!)

Drama in this third sense is not restricted to stage plays, nor even to other media which employ actors. A ballet may have it. Beyond the performing arts, so too may some episode of a novel. That is, we may feel that some part of the action of any story is 'dramatic,' no matter how it is told. But it does not end here. The word is often borrowed to describe real-life situations: a government minister may make a dramatic resignation speech; there may be a dramatic rescue at sea; we may become gripped by the drama of a penalty shoot-out, and so on. Such usage of the word has *some* connection with its application to the action of plays (since the underlying idea in all cases concerns the effect upon an audience), but it is far more important to realize that action can be dramatic in a play which would *not* be counted dramatic if we happened to come across it in real life. Plays (like films) have a strange power to intensify the dramatic quality or effect of the action they present.

In what follows we shall not be concerned with the first sense of drama outlined above, that is, drama as activity, but only with the second and third senses: drama as form and drama as quality of action.

THE DRAMATIC PRESENT

In plays, action is presented *as if it is happening here and now*. This is a basic feature of dramatic form.

It makes no difference to this if the setting of the play is in the past or in the future. Bertolt Brecht's *Mother Courage and Her Children*, for example, is set in the seventeenth century, during the Thirty Years War, but when we see Mother Courage's mute daughter, Kattrin, climb on a roof and start beating a drum to awaken a sleeping town which is about to be attacked, we see this happening as it were in front of our eyes. Similarly, when we read the scene we read dialogue and stage directions which also present this action as happening in the present. It cannot be otherwise. Dramatic action may be *set* in the past or future, but it cannot *take place* in the past or future.

To be more precise, dramatic action cannot *be represented as taking place* in the past or future, for what is present in this way is really a representation of the action. The audience does not actually see Kattrin climbing on to the roof of a house, but an actress playing Kattrin using some part of the stage set in order to represent this action. But while this distinction is both necessary and obvious, it is equally important to stress that in dramatic form *action is represented by means of action!*

More fully, in dramatic form action is *to be* represented by means of action. The 'to be' is necessary if the definition is to apply to play texts as well as to plays in performance. Now, the action (to be) represented is usually fictional while the action which represents it is real, it is what the actors actually do on stage. In reading a play text, most readers will simply try to imagine the former, the fictional action, but a skilled reader will try to imagine the latter, the way this fictional action can be represented on stage.

It is possible, however, for someone to write a text in dramatic form without having any intention that it should be performed. In this case, the reader should obviously imagine the represented action rather than any performance of it. In some such cases, the role played by the reader's imagination in visualizing the scene and characters is minimal or inessential. For example, Plato's Socratic Dialogues are philosophical works where the reader's primary focus is likely to be on the ideas expressed, in spite of the fact that Plato was a skilled prose artist whose characters sometimes seem to 'come to life'.

The fact that a text is written in dramatic form does not mean that it is necessarily dramatic in the third sense of the term outlined above. A transcript of a casual conversation, for example, is very unlikely to be so. In these cases, it is preferable to use the term 'dialogue form'.

Still, a text in dramatic form may be dramatic in the sense that its action and situation (as against its ideas) engages the reader's interest (involving, thus, the third sense of the word) and yet such a text may still not be intended for performance. Robert Browning's poem "My Last Duchess" is a good example. This poem is a dramatic monologue. It is supposedly spoken by the Duke of Ferrara to a visitor, a representative of the father of the Duke's intended second bride, in front of a portrait of his first wife:

> She thanked men, – good! But thanked
> Somehow – I know not how – as if she ranked
> My gift of a nine-hundred-years-old name
> With anybody's gift. Who'd stoop to blame
> This sort of trifling? Even had you skill
> In speech – (which I have not) – to make your will
> Quite clear to such an one, and say, "Just this
> Or that in you disgusts me...."

Here, the rhythms of speech are strong and the Duke's continuing resentment and jealousy of his first wife is clear. Overall, the characterization is deft and the dramatic situation is established with great economy. Yet nothing in the writing or the nature of the text suggests that Browning intended it for performance.

The important issue here is not so much the author's intention as the way that intention affects the nature of the text itself – even, we might say, the way that intention is implicitly 'built into' the text. In the case of Browning's poem there is a certain weak sense in which a performance of it would 'add' something to it, if only a more individual tone of voice, but it is doubtful that any reader reading this poem is going to think, 'I would really like to see this performed'. But just such a thought can easily occur when reading a play. It is as though the poem is 'complete' as a text, even as the text of a dramatic monologue, in a way that most play texts are not.

To put this point another way, it is as though play texts, written in dramatic form, contain some dialogue (and/or monologue), some stage directions and something else which is not written at all, a kind of 'call for performance' or 'need to be performed'. But we cannot say in a few words what it is in play texts that constitutes this 'call for performance'.

It was said in the Introduction that some plays are more 'readable' than others in the sense that their themes, characters, plots and such like can be relatively easily accessed or grasped by a reading (as distinct from watching a performance). We can develop the point by saying that, as a dramatic monologue, "My Last Duchess" has one hundred percent 'readability'. But any dramatic text that seems to the reader such that performance would *enhance* it rather than merely *illustrate* it, in other words one that is written so that it 'calls for' performance, cannot have one hundred percent 'readability'. Nonetheless, the general point holds true that some plays are more easily and fully appreciable by means of reading than others.

DRAMATIC MONOLOGUE VS FIRST PERSON NARRATION

Some novels are written using 'first person narration'. That is, in telling the story the narrator uses the pronoun 'I' as well as 'she' and 'he' because the narrator is – or was – a character, often a principal character, in the story being told. How does this differ from dramatic monologue?

Most, but not all, first person narrations are in the past tense, but so are some dramatic monologues, at least insofar as they too tell some story. In a dramatic monologue, however, even if the main events of the story have already happened and are simply narrated during the monologue, the full or 'true' story cannot be over because the act of narration itself is an event within that story. In a past tense first person narration, on the other hand, the story as such is over and the telling of it is not an act within it. For this reason, the narrator is usually just a voice, not located in any specific place or situation. The only thing that matters about that voice is that it is telling the story. This is not to say, however, that the 'voice' is not given some character in the way it tells the story, for it often is. But character is not enough to establish drama. The speaker of a dramatic monologue, in contrast, not only has a character but exists in a setting and is in a situation that is expressed in the monologue or at least reflected in the way it is spoken. Thus, while a first person narration is usually nothing more than the telling of the story (perhaps with some non-narrative reflections upon it too), a dramatic monologue must always be more than this, for it has to establish precisely the situation within which the monologue is spoken. Moreover, in a true dramatic monologue, this present situation is always more important than the story which is told, for the significance of the story as such lies entirely in the way it leads up to and helps us understand the present situation.

A present tense first person narration is somewhat different. Since it is in the present tense, then necessarily the narration itself has to be understood as taking place within some situation within the story. As a result, it often has some genuinely dramatic qualities. However, in this case the story being told still tends to be what matters most rather than the 'drama' of its telling.

DRAMA AND STORY

Plays tell stories.

We commonly use the verb 'tell' as a synonym for 'narrate,' but plays do not tell stories by means of narration. Even so, we need to keep the verb 'tell' in referring to plays as vehicles for a fiction because it would be a mistake to say instead that plays 'enact' stories. This may seem surprising at first, for the dramatic action of plays is enacted on stage. However, the dramatic action which is enacted is not necessarily the whole story which the play tells.

If a person is asked to tell the story of Oedipus they will probably say something like this…. 'King Laios of Thebes was told by an oracle that he would be killed by his own son. When his wife, Jocasta, gave birth to a boy, Laios ordered that it be taken to Mount Cithairon and killed. But the shepherd who had to carry out this order took pity on the baby and gave it to another shepherd who took it to Corinth where it was adopted by King Polybos and his wife Merope. Much later, Oedipus – for this was how the baby had been named – visited the oracle at Delphi where he was told that his fate was to kill his own father and marry his own mother. Believing his parents to be Polybos and Merope, Oedipus did not return to Corinth but began a life of wandering. One day he was insulted while on the road by an arrogant man, whom he killed, not knowing that this was Laios. Later, Oedipus freed the city of Thebes from the curse of the Sphinx by answering the Sphinx's riddle. As a reward, he was made King of Thebes (since Laios had been reported killed) and given Jocasta as his wife….'

Nearly everything we know of this story comes from Sophocles' play *Oedipus The King*, which was first performed in Athens around 430 BCE. But the action of Sophocles' play begins after the events described above. Oedipus is already King of Thebes and has even had children by his wife-mother. As the play begins, we learn that Thebes is suffering from a terrible plague and that Oedipus has already sent his brother-in-law (and maternal uncle), Creon, to Delphi to learn from the oracle what must be done to save the city. The message which returns is that the murderer of King Laios must be found and punished. Oedipus undertakes to do just that. In consequence, he discovers not only that *he* is the man he is looking for, but also that Laios was his own father and Jocasta is his own mother. He has killed the one and married the other, just as the oracle had predicted years before.

The part of the 'story of Oedipus' which is enacted in the play – or, to put it differently, which is dramatized by Sophocles – is its last part, the 'tip of the iceberg,' and its action occupies only a few hours. But the last part of the story (the dramatized part) has a special function, for it is the part of the story in which the whole story is told. It is the part of Oedipus' story in which Oedipus learns his story.

Notice then that if someone is asked to say what the *plot* of *Oedipus* is, as against the story of Oedipus, they will understand that they are being asked to recount the events which make up the dramatic action of the play rather than the biography of the person (although in spoken language the difference between Oedipus – the person – and *Oedipus* – the play title – is not marked as it is in print). In general we should restrict the term 'plot,' when discussing drama, to the dramatized action so that it is not – or not necessarily – synonymous with 'story'.

Ghosts, by the Norwegian playwright Henrik Ibsen, is similar in the way that the story is bigger than the dramatized action, for this story too includes a past which is revealed throughout the play. It also involves a *discovery* about the past, but one which is rather more complex than in *Oedipus The King*, where Oedipus himself simply discovers the awful truth. (Jocasta discovers it too, of course, earlier than Oedipus, but the focus of the play is not on her.) In *Ghosts*, Mrs Alving reveals the truth about her dead husband's dissolute lifestyle separately to two different characters, firstly (in Act One) to an old friend, Pastor Manders, secondly (in Act Three) to her son, Osvald. Between these confessions she seems to have changed her mind about her late husband's character; the very negative picture she paints for the Pastor is replaced, not much later, by a much more sympathetic portrait for her (and, of course, his) son. It is possible, then, that she has discovered something herself, at least that she has learned to see things differently, although she may simply be trying to protect Osvald from the harsher truth.

The way in which the story may be bigger than the enacted part of it relates to the third sense of drama, drama as a quality of the action. Firstly, plays where this is the case tend to be *climactic* in structure (a feature that will be discussed more fully in Chapter Three). The last part of the story which is enacted in the play is the part where a long sequence of events, linked by cause and effect, is finally coming to a head, in other words, building up to a *climax*. Secondly, where events enacted onstage are seen to be affected by other events which have happened offstage, the effect is often one of *dramatic compression*. The onstage action, that is, is made more complex and more intense by external influences. In relation to this point, note that such external influences need not come from the past, but may arise because of offstage events that take place during the course of the play's action.

DRAMATIC COMPRESSION

Dramatic compression has other sources too and certain exercises used for devising plays can help us understand better this.

Suppose three or four people are asked to create a scene, any scene they like, set anywhere they like, but one in which there must be some tension or conflict between at least two of the characters. They are given five to ten minutes to invent the situation and the characters and to sketch out a rough plan of the scene. They then improvise it. What is likely to happen is that the resulting scene will be very 'wordy'. The performers will tend to keep talking, saying all sorts of unnecessary things, both because it is – or rather it feels – much easier to improvise speech than action and because they believe that words can establish where they are and who they are as well as what is happening between them. To anyone watching, the result is very likely to be boring.

As a next step the performers are told to play the scene again (keeping the same situation, characters and plot), but this time a limit is put on the number of lines that they are allowed to speak. This limit should be strict, maybe ten lines, maybe as few as five. Five minutes or so will be needed to plan this, since the choice of lines is crucial.

The second version is very likely to feel much more *dramatic* than the first. But why? One effect of rationing lines is to force the actors to use actions much more than in the first improvisation in order to communicate where they are, who they are and what is happening between them. Instead of saying "If I don't leave soon I'm never going to get there in time" a performer can look anxiously at her watch. This gives the scene a more multi-layered feel and engages the audience more actively, since spectators enjoy decoding what they see and putting two and two together. But it is probably not the main reason for an increased sense of drama. That lies in the relation between the lines spoken and the scene as a whole.

To understand this, it is worth asking if the result would have been the same if the *initial* instruction had been to improvise the scene with the restricted number of lines. Almost certainly, it would not have been; instead, the result would have been weaker or 'thinner' in some way. When this exercise is done well, the striking thing is that much of what was in the original 'wordy' version is still there in the second laconic version. As a result, the few words that are spoken seem like tips of icebergs and seem to carry so much more significance. The dialogue is something like a 'zip file'.

> Performance 'unzips' a rich and complex scene. Of course, it will not necessarily be the case that compressed dramatic dialogue created in this way would work on the page, that is, that it would suggest the same rich and complex scene if it were first encountered in script form. But that is exactly what we expect good dramatic writing to do. [1]

ONSTAGE AND OFFSTAGE

The dramatized or enacted parts of the story are represented as taking place onstage. Other parts of the story, however, take place offstage. Of course, they do not take place in the actual offstage area of the theatre building, in the wings or dressing rooms! They are assumed to take place in an extension of the imaginary or fictional world of the story, part of which is represented onstage.

Offstage events may have taken place in the past, before the dramatic action itself begins, or they may take place in the present, during the time in which the plot itself takes place.

Plays vary greatly in the extent to which they make use of offstage events. This relates to the *conventions* which the playwright adopts, the 'unwritten rules' of play writing which vary from culture to culture and from period to period. In some plays, for example, such as the so-called 'naturalistic' plays of Ibsen and Strindberg, the onstage action is intended to look as much like real life as possible. This usually entails that the onstage setting is a room, since the stage space itself is 'room-like'. Any events which take place in the street or in a nearby forest will have to take place offstage. Moreover, if the onstage room is to be represented as realistically as possible, fully furnished and decorated, then, for obvious practical reasons, scene changes cannot occur quickly or frequently. This too means that certain events must be left to happen offstage. In contrast, if the conventions adopted allow quick and frequent scene changes and a more 'theatrical' way of staging events, there is less need to leave some of these events out of the dramatized onstage action.

Even so, almost all plays refer to an offstage extension of their fictional worlds. After all, when a character enters or exits they are presumed to have come from or to be going somewhere else in the world of the play, rather than the wings of the theatre. Moreover, characters are commonly made to talk about other characters who are offstage at the time. In fact this is a common way of preparing the ground for the first entrance of a central character. At the beginning of Ibsen's *Hedda Gabler*, Tesman's aunt and her maid appear initially, discussing the recent return of Hedda and Tesman from their honeymoon. Tesman then joins them and further discussion of Hedda occurs. Many hints as to her character have been given and expectations set up before she enters. In a similar way, at the beginning of Lorca's *The House of Bernarda Alba*, the tyrannous character of Bernarda is revealed before her first entrance by both the words and the behaviour of the Maid and Poncia. This device is taken to extremes in Moliere's *Tartuffe*, in which Tartuffe does not make an entrance until Act 3 Scene 2, although his divisive presence in the Orgon household has dominated the play from the

---

[1] A much fuller discussion of this valuable exercise can be found in R.Hahlo and P.Reynolds, *Dramatic Events: How to Run a Successful Workshop*, Faber and Faber, 2000, pp. 21-27

beginning. Moreover, an 'offstage character' need not appear at all, although he affects the action in some way. This is the case with the late Mr Alving in Ibsen's *Ghosts* and Mr Godot in Beckett's *Waiting for Godot*.

> # WRITING EXERCISE:
> ## TWO CHARACTERS TALKING ABOUT A THIRD
>
> Two characters have one relation between them, but three characters have three relations between them. Your task is to write a short scene in which two characters onstage are talking about a third character offstage, who is known to both of them. The content of this scene can be anything you like, but you must try to avoid two potential traps.
>
> Firstly, if you put all the emphasis on creating an interesting image of the offstage character and even of his or her relations with the onstage characters, the result will be flat and undramatic. This is because the drama of any scene is always in its 'onstage reality'. But if you focus on the dramatic interaction of the onstage characters without really relating the third character to this, the result will be weak and one-dimensional. Your goal should be to complicate and intensify the dramatic interaction of the onstage characters through their relations to a third unseen character.
>
> Apart from its usefulness in clarifying the relationship between the onstage and offstage aspects of dramatic fiction, this exercise also helps reveal the importance of *triangles* in drama. Moreover, such triangles very often appear 'one side at a time,' that is, with just two of their component characters onstage at one time.

> ## LANGUAGE AND THE 'OFFSTAGE OF DRAMA'
>
> Consider what a performer can do by means of gesture and mime alone to establish some offstage part of the story. She might shade her eyes and peer into the wings, as though trying to make something out, then back away in apparent fear. She might look at her watch, tapping her foot and acting impatiently, waiting for someone who is late. If we add in sound effects, we can have cars passing 'nearby,' distant gunfire, and so on. But it should be quite obvious that *verbal language* is by far the richest source of the 'offstage of drama'. In fact, it is a crucial and defining feature of human natural language that it allows us to refer to things which are not in our immediate environment at the time. For this reason, the creation of an offstage dimension to the drama is very much the responsibility of the playwright.

THE FUNCTION OF THE MESSENGER

When certain events in the story happen offstage, then, in order that they may be seen to affect the onstage action, they have to be 'revealed' in some way. Commonly, this involves one character reporting what has taken place to one or more other characters. In such a case, we can think of the character who reports the offstage events as functioning as a 'messenger,' although s/he may have other functions within the drama too. For example, in Act Four of Ibsen's *Hedda Gabler*, Brack brings the news of Loevborg's death. He gives one version of the story to Hedda, Tesman and Thea Elvsted, then, a little later when he is alone with Hedda, he tells her a somewhat different, more accurate version, for he had previously altered certain details in order to spare Thea's feelings.

In a case like this, Brack is a 'messenger'. Very often, messengers serve to provide the audience with essential information, but they always do so indirectly, by addressing their news to other characters in the drama, and the audience is equally interested in the effect this news has on them. If, on the other hand, the audience has prior knowledge of the substance of the report, all its interest is in the effect on the listening characters.

Here, we need to distinguish messengers from story-tellers. Both messengers and story-tellers are means of introducing a certain amount of narrative into dramatic form, but story-tellers are able to address the audience directly, which messengers are not. Since this is more a *theatrical* than a *dramatic* device, we shall examine it in Chapter Four.

Unlike a story-teller, a messenger remains entirely within the world of the drama. This means that his or her function as a messenger must be *motivated*. The minimum necessary motivation is simply that the messenger has been given a message to take, as in the case of the Boy who tells Estragon and Vladimir that Godot cannot come that day, but will surely come the next, at the end of both acts of Beckett's *Waiting for Godot*. Such a messenger has no initiative of his own. Actual messengers, who are common in ancient Greek tragedy (where it was a convention that no violent action could be represented, but had to be reported), are sometimes like this. If they have not actually been instructed to take a message by a social superior, they may realize for themselves that it is their duty to do so. But beyond this minimum requirement, they are often given some kind of involvement in or relation to the substance of their message. This can take different forms, worth outlining here since they recur in one way or another in later drama.

Firstly, ancient messengers are often 'emotionally involved' in what they report. A fine example is the Herald's speech in Aeschylus' *Agamemnon*. Home again after ten years fighting in the Trojan War, the Herald experiences and 're-lives' a complex set of emotions as he tells of the hardships and horrors of war, the joys of the Greek victory, and the sadness at the loss of comrades on the return voyage.

Secondly, a messenger who reports what another character has done can become a kind of onstage 'representative' of that character, minimally 'enacting' the latter's story while narrating it. This occurs, for example, in Sophocles' *Oedipus the King* where the Messenger, a servant in the palace, reports that Jocasta has hanged herself and that Oedipus has blinded himself. He does so by providing such a detailed and emotive account, including quotations of Oedipus' words, that it has to be 'half-acted' as well.

WRITING EXERCISE:
THE MESSENGER 1

This first messenger exercise is somewhat easier than the second one below. The given situation is as follows. A father has just returned from the public gallery of a law court where his son is on trial for a serious crime. His wife is too upset by the situation to attend the court herself. Therefore her husband must tell her what has happened in court that day. To make this scene work as drama, much more is required than the messenger's 'message,' however interesting the day's court proceedings may be. What is the mother's attitude and what are her reactions? How do her attitude and reactions affect the way the father tells the story? And how does this reveal his attitude? You will probably find that there needs to be some kind of conflict of attitudes between the mother and father. There may be things she doesn't want to hear but that he wants her to hear, and other things he doesn't want to reveal but which she feels she has to know.

WRITING EXERCISE:
THE MESSENGER 2

This second messenger exercise aims to develop a different, more 'theatrical' device in which the messenger becomes a kind of actor within the drama. The messenger here should not be involved in the given situation in the same way or to the same extent that the father is involved in the exercise above. However, as s/he reports what has taken place, s/he is transformed *to some extent* into the person whose story she is telling. For this to occur, there must be some dissolving of the boundary between two different places and two different times. The goal is to make the report 'come to life' as if it is no longer a mere report, although that is ultimately what it remains. Insofar as this is achieved, the listener – who should of course be personally involved in what has happened – becomes not just a listener to a report but *more like* a witness to the actual event. However, you must not push the transformation so far that the audience actually comes to believe that it is now witnessing the original scene. The messenger must remain a messenger throughout. But s/he is a messenger with a strange power to make the message come to life.

Here, the choice of subject matter is crucial. Suppose the message concerns a character called Frank. It is best if the report contains some speeches of Frank's that can be quoted. But if Frank is merely reported as having said certain things, there will be little dramatic interest.

This exercise is related to an essay called "The Street Scene" in which Bertolt Brecht argues that theatre can be usefully compared to the way a witness to a traffic accident tells others what he saw. For example, such a witness may say, "Just before the impact, I saw the driver turn to his companion" – and as he says this he turns his own head. Such enactments have special significance for they serve to emphasize what is truly important in the action being reported. In this exercise, however, you should push the enactment somewhat further than this.

Thirdly and lastly, a messenger may become 'entangled' in the plot, while continuing to represent another 'level,' like an alternative or counterpoint to the world of the main action. The only full or true example of this in ancient drama is the Guard in Sophocles' *Antigone*, who reports that someone has performed forbidden funeral rites for Polyneices, in a scene which is one of the most remarkable in all ancient tragedy. The guard is aware that the bearers of bad news are unwelcome. But he is not prepared for the fact that Creon goes on to accuse him and his comrades of some complicity in the unlawful act, threatening them with very severe reprisals if they fail to bring the culprit to him. This provokes the Guard to stand up for himself and even to engage boldly in argument with Creon. Throughout, the Guard is characterized by a clumsy form of speech which makes him seem akin to the lower class characters in Shakespeare. This is unique in Greek tragedy, where the prevailing convention is that all characters, whatever their social status, speak a dignified, heightened language appropriate to the genre. The effect is strangely comical, yet wins the audience to the Guard's side. It is as though Sophocles uses this scene to draw our attention to an alternative world, one which may get caught up in the events of tragedy but which does not really belong to the 'world of tragedy' or share in the 'tragic world view,' and in doing this he even comes close to subverting the sense of the 'tragic' in his own play!

We can distinguish between the strict motivation of the messenger – the reason for bringing the message – and her or his degree and kind of involvement in the drama. The Guard, we can say, is a messenger first, one who becomes involved in the drama secondarily and on the basis of his primary function. In *Hedda Gabler*, on the other hand, Brack is first and foremost involved in the drama, albeit as a secondary character, and takes on the temporary function of messenger in a way that relates to his involvement. This gives him two levels of motivation in bringing the bad news. On the first superficial level he is simply performing a kind of social duty. On the second level, however, he is letting Hedda know that he now knows what has previously happened between her and Loevborg, in particular that she has given the latter one of her pistols with which to shoot himself. Brack's intention here is to use this information, which would be scandalous if publicly known, to blackmail her into an affair with him.

Messengers are only one manifestation of a more general feature of drama. This is the need to provide the audience with the information necessary to understand the situation within which drama arises. Narrative fiction can provide that information directly by means of the narrative, although of course readers can also 'pick up' certain things from the words and perhaps even the actions of the characters. But in drama, the information which is necessary to understand a situation tends to be generated from within and as part of that very situation. Moreover, audiences tend to expect information to arise 'naturally' and even incidentally, not to be openly and obviously provided as information. This is particularly true of more modern plays, especially those that adopt more or less naturalistic conventions. However, since the problem of providing information is most acute at the beginning of a play, during the so-called *exposition* phase of the plot, some earlier plays adopt the very convenient device of a Prologue. This is a speech commonly (but not always) delivered direct to the audience which sets the scene and outlines the story so far. What is interesting about this device is that the audience readily understands that although direct address and open provision of information are permitted here at the very beginning, they will not be permitted afterwards.

> ## WRITING EXERCISE:
> ### 'A CONVERSATION OVERHEARD ON A BUS'
>
> Imagine two people talking about a subject which is familiar to them both. You may imagine that you are sitting behind them on a bus, but this is not essential. What is important is that *they* do not need to tell each other what it is they are talking about, since they both know this. Moreover, they both know that they both know it. It would be quite unnatural for these two to talk in such a way that a third party or eavesdropper (an audience in other words) would be provided with all necessary background information to understand the conversation. But does an audience *need* to know this? *How much* does it need to know? And *when* does it need to find out? These questions can be explored by writing such a dialogue. You can try to do this so as to make the subject become clear to an audience, at some point in the dialogue, without its ever being explicitly mentioned, and you can try to do it so that the subject remains hidden throughout. In the latter case, will the audience be frustrated or even more interested? (Note that a lot will depend on the choice of subject, for some kinds of subject are much more easily guessable than others.)
>
> This exercise (which concerns the relationship between the offstage and the onstage, but here without any messenger) reveals two things about drama. In the first place, it demonstrates that – at least in a certain kind of play – information given to the audience must always be motivated. In this kind of play, the audience will feel alienated and even patronized if information is obviously written into the dialogue solely for its benefit, without being dramatically motivated ("Have you heard about Jill?" – "You mean have I heard about her husband's affair? Yes, I have"). Secondly, it reveals that audiences enjoy the challenge of working things out for themselves. Some information is essential, of course, but the audience's real interest is always in what is actually happening between the onstage characters. This interest can be sustained and even enhanced by withholding information, at least for a time.

CONFLICT

It is often claimed that the essence of drama – in its sense as a certain quality of the action – is *conflict*. Conflict is intrinsically dynamic, since it implies a changing, evolving relation between the forces that are in conflict, with one or other gaining the upper hand, maybe in turns. In this way, conflict can drive the plot. The resolution of the plot, moreover, can take the form of the victory of one side and the defeat of the other.

The problem with this idea, at least with the rather simple outline of it just given, is that it brings to mind something like a Superman movie. Serious drama often seems rather different, at least more complex. Consider Shakespeare's *King Lear*, for example. There is a great deal of conflict in this play, most obviously between Lear on the one hand and his daughters Goneril and Regan on the other. But is such conflict the *essence* of this play? Is it not rather a *means* to reveal something else, the truth and complexity of character and even, perhaps, deeper truths about human existence? Is an audience watching *King Lear* gripped only by the questions of who will win and how?

It will help if we make a distinction between *external* and *internal* conflict. External conflict arises between different characters but internal conflict arises within a single character. The 'essence' of the play *King Lear* lies surely in the dramatic power of the scenes on the heath where Lear's madness expresses an internal conflict so terrific and far-reaching that it is echoed in a fearful storm. This internal conflict, of course, has been precipitated by the external conflict with his daughters, but its scope goes way beyond what is at stake there.

Nonetheless, in many plays straightforward external conflict, leading to the victory of one side and the defeat of the other, lends obvious dramatic intensity to the action. In Strindberg's *The Father*, for example, a husband and wife struggle for control over their daughter's education. Behind this struggle lies an incompatibility of world views. The Captain is a scientific rationalist. His wife Laura is religious and narrow minded. She is also the stronger character and she succeeds in reducing her husband to apparent insanity. Edward Albee's *Who's Afraid of Virginia Woolf* also dramatizes marital conflict. Here, Martha taunts and humiliates her husband, George, in front of guests, causing George finally to retaliate in kind. He therefore 'kills' their imaginary son as a way of making Martha face reality.

Frederico Garcia Lorca's *The House of Bernarda Alba* is an excellent example of how a core conflict ripples outwards and generates other conflicts. The tyrannical matriarch, Bernarda, dominates her five unmarried daughters and her servants. This causes internal conflicts in the daughters and conflicts between them, especially when a man courts the eldest, Angustias. Only Adela, the youngest, dares to stand up to her mother, but her rebellion fails and she commits suicide. Note, then, that what Lorca dramatizes here is not simply a conflict between persons, but one between the strict and repressive social control of women on the one hand and erotic desire on the other, for Adela is in love. Bernarda and Adela are respectively the *agents* of these greater forces, while the other conflicts within and between the sisters are *displacements* of this true conflict.

Conflict may be central to drama, but it is not necessarily central to *a play*. Shakespeare's *The Tempest*, for example, contains very little true conflict and what conflict there is in it, such as in Caliban's impotent rebellion against Prospero, is inessential. True conflict implies some kind of balance, if not full equality, between the competing forces. How can this arise where one character, Prospero, is in full control of everything that happens in the play by virtue of his magic powers? We might argue, then, that *The Tempest* is not very 'dramatic'. Its value lies more in its 'theatrical' aspect (all the more so because the 'theatrical' can be equated with the 'magical' here). Even so, there is much more to *The Tempest* than effects and spectacle. Thematically, it is a play about forgiveness and redemption, the very opposite of conflict and even the opposite of victory and defeat insofar as these are the natural ends of conflict. While Prospero 'wins' in one sense, by getting what he wants, he does so without there being any losers!

Some people will be dissatisfied with the conclusion that *The Tempest* is theatrically but not dramatically effective, continuing to feel that it has a certain kind of dramatic interest after all. To admit this, we need to argue that the essence of drama is not so much conflict as *transformation*. Certain characters, or perhaps the situation they are in, are different in some way at the end of the play than they were at the beginning. Conflict is just one, relatively common means of effecting such a transformation. What is extraordinary about *The Tempest* and Shakespeare's other late, great play, *The Winter's Tale*, lies in the nature of the transformation which is dramatized, for it involves a kind of 'erasure of the past'.

A situation is arrived at in which no bitterness at or regret for past wrongs remains, as though it is possible in some strange (magical) way to go back in time and undo evil, though the paradox is that this 'erasure of time' would not be possible if it were not for the passage of time itself. This is most movingly 'dramatized' – or staged – at the end of *The Winter's Tale* when the statue of Hermione 'comes to life' and she is restored to her husband, Leontes, a man whose jealous fantasies some sixteen years earlier had led to what seemed her death. Although an extraordinarily effective theatrical moment (though critics in some periods thought it was evidence of Shakespeare having 'gone soft'), there is certainly also something *dramatic* in this, which cannot adequately be explained in terms of conflict, not even as the resolution of conflict.

Even if we extend our sense of what constitutes drama in this way, we still need to accept that not all plays – indeed, not all dramas – are 'dramatic'. In Beckett's *Waiting for Godot,* for example, there is neither conflict (at least, of any significance) nor transformation. Instead, Vladimir and Estragon do nothing but wait for the arrival of a man who they believe, or hope, will take over from them the responsibility for all their choices. He does not come. They use or waste their freedom of action waiting for someone to come to whom to give their freedom of action away. This play, in fact, can be described as a kind of 'anti-drama'. In this, however, it is not so exceptional as might be thought, but rather the end product of an almost inevitable process. To understand this, recall something that was said earlier. Certain events can seem dramatic in a play, in the sense of the word that denotes a certain quality of action, which would not be counted as 'dramatic' in real life. Once playwrights became aware of this, it became tempting to them, at least to some of them, to try to push it as far as they could.

Crucial in this story is Anton Chekhov. In his last and arguably his greatest play, *The Cherry Orchard*, Chekhov finally succeeded in the goal he had set himself some years before of 'banishing the pistol shot from the stage'. This is literally true, since *The Seagull, Uncle Vanya* and *Three Sisters* all have pistol shots, but *The Cherry Orchard* does not. Its fuller significance, however, lies in the transformation of the nature of plot and especially of climax necessary to achieve it. Chekhov's goal, in fact, was the creation of a new kind of drama in which nothing obviously dramatic happens.

Chekhov succeeds in this in *The Cherry Orchard* by means of a mixture of devices that together create a 'displacement' of the very idea of action. We get the sense that the real story this play tells is not after all the story of the characters who appear onstage, but the story of the cherry orchard itself. This story, moreover, is representative of something larger, the onward march of history. The characters we meet are affected or touched by this, but they are not really part of it. History involves change. These characters do not change, though they grow older.

The basic plot is as follows. The indebted family will soon be forced to auction the cherry orchard if money cannot be raised by some other means. Lopakhin, a successful but kindly businessman, the son of a peasant, advises Ranyevskaia to chop down the orchard and lease the land for holiday villas for the rising middle classes, for he sees in this strategy – no doubt correctly – the only possible economically viable future. She will hear none of this, preferring to live a few more weeks in her own rapidly disappearing world. At the end of the play, the orchard is sold and we hear the sound of axes as the family packs up and leaves.

Although this plot *suggests* in itself the way the characters are 'left out by history,' Chekhov uses several other devices that enhance the effect. Firstly, he weaves together several different plot lines, each involving different characters, such that the play keeps shifting back and forth between them. The effect of this is to make them all seem inconsequential, all the more so in that some are treated quite comically. Secondly, he introduces characters and situations that never seem to change, except by growing older. Indeed, at the very beginning of the play, when she has just returned from years away in Paris, Ranyevskaia's first words are "The nursery!" as she recognizes the room where she used to sleep as a child. Lastly, Chekhov gives certain characters fixed mannerisms, to which they return again and again. Most notably, Gayev is always pretending to pot billiard balls. The latter device is especially interesting. August Strindberg, in his *Preface to Miss Julie*, had condemned this kind of characterization (at least in non-comic plays), and rightly so – for it is clearly an over-simplification of human beings. But what Chekhov achieves with a character like Gayev is the complex sense that the character has simplified himself!

Most importantly, the action of *The Cherry Orchard* proceeds – if that is the right word – *by an evasion of conflict*. In this, Chekhov shifts the focus of the drama away from plot and on to *situation*. In this sense, Chekhov is the true precursor of Samuel Beckett.

Lastly, the common association of drama and conflict may reflect a western bias. Certain Asian traditions, such as Japanese Noh theatre, seem to value other aspects of theatrical imitation and representation, such as the power of plays to create beauty or to evoke sympathetic moods in the audience. Here we shall briefly consider the early and very fine Sanskrit play, *The Recognition of Sankuntala*, by Kalidasa (written at some time between 200 BCE and 600 CE), which enacts a story in which King Dusyanta marries Sakuntala, but is then caused to forget both the marriage and his wife by a curse. The curse can only be broken if Sakuntala shows Dusyanta the ring he has given her as a love token, but she loses this during her journey to his court. He then rejects her, though she is pregnant. Later, the ring is found by a fisherman and taken to the King. He finds Sakuntala living with their son.

We can easily recognize in this brief synopsis a familiar pattern of *complication* leading to a *climax*, Sakutala's rejection, followed by *denouement*. We might also say that there is conflict between Dusyanta and Sakuntala in Act Five, when he fails to recognize her. But this is only momentary; once she is rejected, Sakuntala does not persist in trying to convince him but leaves. The turning point in the resolution of the plot, moreover, does not come from any action of any of the principal characters, but is perfectly accidental – a fisherman finds the ring in the body of a carp. The curse itself is also an 'outside influence,' and has nothing to do with what we normally think of as 'motivation'. Thus, although the two central characters have desires, the plot is far from being simply driven by their desires, and certainly not by any conflict between them.

From the point of view of the Sanskrit dramatist, the plot is not important in itself and has none of the primary importance that Aristotle claimed for it in the *Poetics*. It is one element among others which are combined in the creation of a mood, or *rasa*, appropriate to the subject matter of the play – in this case, the erotic *rasa*. According to the *Natyasastra*, a 'Drama Manual' which is believed to be contemporary with Kalidasa's play, *all* the elements of the play, including not just the story and dramatized action but also poetry, movement, gesture and music must be combined in a unified whole in order to create this mood in the audience. The emphasis here on the combination and synthesis of elements is quite different from Aristotle's analytical approach in which he distinguishes the different component parts of tragedy and ranks them in terms of the importance of their contribution to the 'tragic effect'.

QUESTIONS TO ASK ABOUT YOUR SET PLAYS

1. What is the relationship between the onstage action or plot and the story? Are these identical, or does the story involve more incidents and events than the plot?
2. What, if anything, has happened in the past, i.e. before the play's action begins, which is essential for an understanding of the play? How does the audience learn of it?
3. Does any character discover something about the past? How does this happen? What effects does it have?
4. What events are presumed to happen offstage during the course of the action? Why has the playwright not staged these events?
5. Do any characters function as 'messengers' by bringing information about offstage events to other characters? If so, what is their relation to the message they bring? And what is their motivation for bringing the message?
6. Are important characters referred to and discussed by others before their first entrance? If so, what expectations does this set up in the audience?
7. Are there any 'characters' who affect the onstage action in some way but who never appear onstage themselves?
8. Other than by the use of 'messengers,' how does the playwright communicate essential information about the dramatic situation to the audience, especially in the early stages of the play? How is the communication of this information motivated?
9. How docs the playwright attempt to capture the audience's interest early in the play?
10. What conflicts exist between characters?
11. What conflicts exist within characters?
12. How does conflict contribute to the development of the action?
13. Do conflicts between characters reflect conflicts between wider forces?
14. If conflict is not the focus of interest in the play, what is?

CHAPTER TWO
THE 'PERSONS OF THE DRAMA'

Usually, we talk about the 'characters' in a play. The title of this chapter, however, is a translation of the Latin phrase *Dramatis Personae*, which is sometimes found at the beginning of play texts above the list of the names or identities of the characters. Still, the 'persons of the drama' not only sounds a little odd, but, as a translation, it also misses something, for *persona* means a mask in Latin. It would be more accurate to translate the phrase as 'the roles of the drama'. A role is something that we 'play,' whether onstage or in life. It is something 'taken on,' rather than the whole of a person's character or self. A role is also often a contributory part of a whole beyond the person who takes it on; we can say, for example, that 'his role in the company's success has been great'. In the same way, a role in a play is also a 'part' in the play, a contribution to the play as a whole.

We tend to use the terms 'role' or 'part' when we are talking about the play as something to be performed, preferring the word 'character' when we are discussing it as a fiction. It is the same word, of course, that we use when discussing other types of fiction, such as the novel. The problem with this word, at least in relation to drama, is that it tends to make us think about characters in terms of their 'individual personalities' rather than their function in the play. To call a part in a play a 'character' is implicitly to lift that part out of the play, as though it has some kind of life of its own. This reflects the modern interest in psychology and the cultural value placed on individuality. It also reflects our assumption that rounded or 'three-dimensional' characters are artistically superior to flat or 'two-dimensional' ones. All this can lead us to overlook certain features of how plays work.

Still, if we ought at least to be careful in the way we use the term 'character,' we should also recognize that the basic subject matter of all drama is people. We watch plays because we are interested in people. We are interested in people because, to greater or lesser extent, all people – including fictional people – are *like us*. (Moreover, because we are a complicated species, some of the examples used in this chapter are developed at some length!)

In a novel, the author can take the reader 'inside the head' of a character to witness his thoughts. The narrator in a novel can also tell the reader what a character is feeling or what her motivation is. More generally, the novel form gives equal access to the subjective inner life (the mental world) and the objective outer life (the behaviour in an interpersonal or social context) of characters. In plays, quite differently, the objective outer life of characters is dominant. This does not mean that the audience is expected to be interested only or even primarily in this outer life. On the contrary, an interest in people is always an interest in how they think and feel as well as in what they do. What it does mean is that the audience (or reader) of a play largely has to construct the inner life on the evidence of the outer life. It is true, of course, that characters in plays sometimes think aloud – as, for example, in Hamlet's famous soliloquy, "To be, or not to be…" – and they may describe their thoughts and feelings to others, but the general rule in drama is that the audience has access to the inner life of characters *through* their outer life.

Before we go on to analyze this more fully, it will be useful to consider the different types of characters that can exist in plays, not in the sense of different 'psychological types' but of different kinds of roles or parts that characters can play in the whole.

THE CLASSIFICATION OF CHARACTERS

Firstly, and on a very basic level, a character in a play either participates in the dramatic action, however indirectly or marginally, or does not. The latter case is relatively rare. It arises most often when one character is a story-teller and the other characters exist within the story which is told. Note though that story-tellers sometimes move into and out of the stories they tell, participating in them briefly in order to make sure the story turns out correctly! Occasionally, certain characters do not participate in the dramatic action for other reasons. Caryl Churchill's *Vinegar Tom* is the story of a witch hunt in seventeenth century rural England. This drama occupies twenty short scenes. The twenty-first scene which follows is not part of the dramatized story at all. Instead, the authors of a famous fifteenth century book on witchcraft, the *Malleus Maleficarum,* two Dominican friars called James Sprenger and Heinrich Kramer, appear on stage to explain to the audience why women are more likely than men to become witches, but they do this as if playing a comic double act in an old fashioned variety show! These characters are part of the play, but they do not participate in the drama. Nor do they even belong to the world of the drama. A somewhat different example is the figure of the Moon in Act 3, Scene 1 of Lorca's *Blood Wedding*. That the Moon should appear like this, speaking verse, is essential to Lorca's intention to transcend the social world in which the drama is born, raising the play to a more metaphysical level. Lorca's Moon desires the warmth and the colour of blood, through the deaths of Leonardo and the Bridegroom, but this desire is not an active force within the drama. Rather, it seems to be intended as a symbol of the way in which the main characters are in the grip of something greater even than their own desires.

Secondly, a character who participates in the drama tends to be either proactive or reactive within that drama. A proactive character is one whose actions cause the plot to advance in some way by bringing about some change in the situation. Anything done by a reactive character does not cause the plot to advance like this. Now, this distinction is useful only if it is strictly interpreted. Most proactive characters will also react to events at points in the drama, and their own plot-advancing actions may be reactions to something which precedes them. But they are not to be called reactive characters. A reactive character is reactive throughout, never proactive. The chorus is ancient Greek tragedy is reactive in this sense. So is the 'fat Brahmin,' Vidusaka, in Kalidasa's *The Recognition of Sakuntala*. Moreover, proactivity is strictly defined in terms of its effects on the plot. Hamlet, for example, consistently fails to carry out the revenge which he feels duty-bound to do, until the very end of the play. The consequences of his 'inaction' are great. His 'inaction,' in fact, is a kind of action, and as such it is entirely proactive, since it is what, in part, advances the plot. His friend, Horatio, on the other hand, has an entirely reactive role. Note then that reactive characters very often have the function of *confidants*, as do Vidusaka and Horatio; proactive characters confide in them, thereby revealing essential information to the audience.

Thirdly, a proactive character is either *static* or *developing* (while reactive characters are always static). Static characters are the same at the end of the play as they are at the beginning. Developing characters, on the other hand, change or grow in some way, often as a result of some kind of learning process. Kattrin, in Brecht's *Mother Courage and her Children*, develops to the point at which she acts heroically to try to save a town. But Mother Courage herself is static. Brecht underlines this at the end of the play by having Mother Courage exit pulling her wagon and calling to soldiers to take her with them, exactly as she has done for so many years, even though she has lost all her children to war, one by one, through the course of the play.

However, this last distinction is not always so clear-cut. Sometimes a character does not exactly develop; instead, more and more of their 'true character' is revealed as the action progresses. After all, different sides of anyone's character will be revealed in different circumstances. Sometimes this process might yet be counted as 'development,' but this may come down to a matter of opinion or interpretation. In Shakespeare's *Measure for Measure*, Angelo is initially a man of the strictest moral principle. Finding himself sexually attracted to Isabella, who comes to him to plead for her brother's life (her brother, Claudio, is under sentence of death for having impregnated his fiancée), Angelo 'turns into' a villain, offering to grant her plea only if she will "lay down the treasures of [her] body" to him. In one sense, Angelo was not, after all, the man of virtue that he seemed to be. Looked at this way, his true character has simply been revealed. But in another sense, he was a man of virtue who has now 'fallen'. He is certainly not like Moliere's Tartuffe, a pure hypocrite. When he finds himself tempted by Isabella, he struggles with himself and expresses self-disgust. In a case like this, the question of whether we witness character-development or character-revelation should be decided on the basis of which interpretation makes the most interesting drama.

Apart from these distinctions, we also need to distinguish between primary and secondary characters, or (what is basically the same thing) between central and peripheral characters. But while often necessary, this is a very crude categorization. For one thing, any and all non-primary characters tend to be called 'secondary,' a 'catch-all' term which fails to recognize that there may be further distinction, a third level of importance, perhaps, or even a fourth. Furthermore, characters can be 'secondary' in different ways. A character may be of secondary importance in relation to the plot, but of major importance in relation to the play's themes, or vice versa. The same applies, obviously enough, to the term 'peripheral'.

In discussing primary characters, the terms 'protagonist' and 'antagonist' are often used. These terms are not always appropriate, at least if they are understood in their root senses. A 'protagonist' is a 'first or primary contestant,' that is, one involved in a contest or struggle. An 'antagonist' is an opponent in such a struggle. If this description fits, the terms are useful. As for the term 'hero,' it is commonly used as a simple synonym for 'central character,' since very few plays have heroism in the true or original sense of the word as their theme.

Lastly, note that many plays written from the 1960s onwards were written for (and sometimes with) specific theatre groups which had a progressive, democratic ethos and which were trying to break down some of the hierarchies of traditional theatre. Such groups did not have 'leading ladies' (or men), nor did they have novice actors who would be glad of a 'walk on' or 'bit' part. Hence plays written for such groups often attempt to give relatively equal roles to the actors (though sometimes they do so by giving several roles to one actor, a performance device called 'doubling') and this tends to break down the distinction between primary and secondary characters which is so evident in more traditional theatre.

Caryl Churchill's *Vinegar Tom* is an example; it was written for and with the feminist theatre group, Monstrous Regiment. While, in a sense, this play has a central character – Alice – it does so only insofar as Alice appears to be relatively modern in spirit (the play being set in the seventeenth century) and so functions as a kind of 'way into' the play for the modern audience, someone with whom spectators can identify. This kind of centrality is quite unlike that in Ibsen's *Hedda Gabler*, where the different characters can be diagrammatically arranged in a pyramid, with Hedda alone at the top.

OBJECTIVES AND SUPER-OBJECTIVES

When an actor has to play a character in a play, s/he will usually ask 'What does this character want?' This question can be asked of a specific scene – What is the character trying to get at this point in the play? – or of the play as a whole. In Konstantin Stanislavski's system of acting, what a character is trying to get at some specific point in a play is called that character's *objective*, while their *super-objective* is what they want overall, that which ultimately motivates everything they do in the course of the play.

IMPROVISATION: 'BREAKFAST TIME'

This exercise, which is used in drama workshops to bring out some important aspects of devising, is useful in demonstrating the value of objectives.

Three performers are asked to improvise a scene at the breakfast table. They are having breakfast and they are allowed to talk only about what they are eating and drinking. Such a scene is obviously boring and lacks all drama. They are then asked to play the scene again, but one of them, let's say Beth, is first taken aside and told that she is in love with Joe. Neither Joe nor Will knows this. The rule is the same – the only topic of conversation is breakfast – but Beth now tries to communicate her love to Joe in the way she offers him more coffee and comments on how 'fruity' the marmalade is. Will, of course, now feels left out and he expresses this in the irritated *way* he asks Beth why the butter is hard. We now have a drama, one which has arisen entirely because one character has an objective. However, this objective does not appear in the 'script,' that is in the words spoken. It is entirely in the *subtext*, a concept that will be explained later in this chapter.

There is a good reason for this way of approaching characters in plays, and it holds for the student of drama as literature as much as it does for the actor. **Plays consist of actions, actions tend to be motivated, and motives tend to be desires**. Notice, then, that this formulation provides the basic explanation of how the inner life of a character, his or her desires, is related to and expressed through that character's outer life, his or her actions.

However, although the question – 'What does this character want?' – is easy to ask, it is not always easy to answer. What, for example, is Hedda Gabler's super-objective, or Hamlet's? In cases like these, the difficulty of determining the super-objective is closely related to the complexity of the character and, from an actor's point of view, the desirability of the role.

CASE STUDY: WHAT DOES HEDDA GABLER REALLY WANT?

Hedda Gabler is a young woman of aristocratic background who has recently married the middle class George Tesman, an unimaginative, rather homely academic. They are not at all well matched and live in a house which Hedda had once casually and untruly told him she admired, merely to make conversation when George was tongue-tied. Hedda is now pregnant, but detests both the pregnancy itself and the thought of being responsible for a child. So far in this account, Hedda seems defined by what she does *not* want. Although she married Tesman, she hardly wants him as a husband and certainly does not love him (to her, love is a "sickly word"); she had and has no real desire to live in the house he has found for her; lastly, she dislikes intensely the traditional female role of motherhood.

Early in the play, it is suggested that Hedda wants a certain kind of conventional social life, gatherings and witty conversations with people of her own kind. That she should be able to enjoy this is, in fact, a term of her agreement to marry. But as the play progresses it becomes quite clear that this is not what she truly wants. It is an entirely superficial desire and an indicator that she has settled for 'second best' in her life.

Matters would remain much like this, with Hedda in an awful but (for a woman) not uncommon trap, were it not for the arrival of Eilert Loevborg on the scene. Loevborg is an intellectual of genius and a recently reformed alcoholic. Years before, he and Hedda had enjoyed a kind of intimacy, which had ended with Hedda threatening to kill him with one of her father's pistols. It is clear that Loevborg is still strongly drawn to Hedda. She, however, would never consider leaving her husband for fear of scandal; nor would she engage in any extra-marital affair.

Loevborg has been helped in overcoming his alcoholism and in returning to writing by Thea Elvsted, the young wife of an elderly magistrate. Thea, in contrast to Hedda, is prepared to leave her husband and has in fact done so in order to pursue Loevborg to the town, fearful that he may fall back into his old dissolute ways. Learning of this, Hedda becomes jealous of the influence Thea has had over Loevborg. Firstly, and in front of Thea, she engineers a situation in which Loevborg begins drinking again, by revealing to him Thea's fears about him. Secondly, she destroys the only manuscript of his book, a book written with Thea's assistance. As she does so, she says that she is burning Thea's "child". When Loevborg comes to her in despair, believing he has lost his manuscript when drunk, Hedda gives him one of her father's pistols with which to shoot himself and tells him to "do it beautifully".

In her jealousy, what Hedda wants is to destroy Thea's influence over Loevborg and its 'fruit,' the book. But the only way in which she can 'take Thea's place' by substituting her own influence over him for Thea's is by helping him to kill himself. Here, she expresses what she seems to believe is her true desire, the desire to have some control over a man's destiny. That this control should manifest itself so perversely follows from the fact that it seems never to enter Hedda's head that she might return to a relationship with Loevborg.

However, if an actress were to be content with this account of Hedda's 'true desire,' the resulting performance of the part would very likely fail to engage the audience's sympathy with Hedda and would fail to uncover the full significance of the play. In other words, what Hedda thinks she really wants is not what she really wants. Hedda's true desire is very deeply buried and she is largely unconscious of it.

The problem here is related to the way the dramatic action is rooted in a longer story, one extending back into the past, a relatively common feature of plays that was discussed in the preceding chapter. Hedda's true desire, that is, was expressed in her original relationship with Loevborg. Everything that follows the breaking of that relationship tends to be either a compensation for or a perversion of that desire. Hence, while Hedda's various *objectives* can be found in the dramatized action, her *super-objective* has to be understood both from this action and from earlier, undramatized events.

In preparing a production of *Hedda Gabler*, in fact, it would be a good idea to improvise around the earlier scene which is only briefly described in the play itself. Through the play, we learn that Hedda and Loevborg used to sit together, in the presence of her father, pretending to read an illustrated magazine while he quietly told her all about his various excesses. Hedda herself, we learn, was not simply a passive audience, but questioned him, indirectly yet unambiguously, seeking to know as much as possible of a forbidden world. Then, when at a later stage Loevborg expressed a physical desire for her, she felt that he was betraying their 'comradeship'. It was then that she threatened to kill him with the pistol and a little later, as she admits, considered turning it upon herself.

What exactly did Hedda want *at that time*? Loevborg claims that it was "life". If so, such a desire cannot be satisfied vicariously or voyeuristically, through the mere narration of someone else's adventures. But there is no suggestion that Hedda would have liked to live that kind of life herself. Far from it. By reason of her sex and social rank, Hedda's world was highly restricted and limited. What she wanted was to *see* beyond those restrictions and limitations – but not to *go* beyond them. In part, this explains her rejection of Loevborg's physical advances. But it does not explain her sense that he had betrayed her, as revealed by her extreme reaction. At the core of the problem, in fact, is Hedda's rejection of her own sexuality, something which lies behind her 'denial' of her pregnancy too. Loevborg had seemed a 'comrade' to her only when and insofar as he had seemed like an accomplice in this rejection of the 'basely physical,' even, ironically, as he told her of his own physical depravities. This rejection, in Hedda's case, expresses a desire for something finer, more 'beautiful' in life, without knowing exactly what this might be. And this *is* her deepest desire, still evident at times in the play, so that her story – and her tragedy – can only be one of cruel disillusionment. Since there *is* nothing finer or more beautiful in life (even Loevborg's death turning out to be messy and sordid), Hedda kills herself. Her suicide is simultaneously a defeat – for she has seen that life holds nothing beautiful for her – and a victory – for she at least kills herself 'beautifully' with a shot through the temple. The only way, it seems, that Hedda can get what she really wants is through death.

Hedda is an especially complex case and, as a result, one of the great female roles. It is generally easier to say what a character 'really wants'. Even so, we must be careful not to over-simplify. Macbeth, for example, wants to become king. But this should be seen as a manifestation of a deeper desire, one which is less easy to specify. Richard, Duke of Gloucester, (in Shakespeare's *Richard III*) wants to become king too, but without this being a manifestation of any deeper desire (although it involves some compensation for his being a hunchback). In Macbeth's case it is more like a desire to 'be something more than he is,' which happens, in the specific circumstances and under the prompting of Lady Macbeth, to lead to regicide. To put this differently, had Macbeth lived in a different, later and freer world, he might have channeled his ambition into becoming a great explorer or a great scientist. But confined by the rigid feudal structure of his world he can only rise criminally. We do not feel this 'extra dimension' of a malcontent like Richard.

ACTIONS SPEAK LOUDER THAN WORDS

In relation to everyday life, the phrase 'actions speak louder than words' is used to point out that mere verbal claims, for example to support some cause, are worth little compared to actual deeds. One's actions may confirm one's words (or claims), or contradict them. Either way, it is the actions which 'tell the truth'. Since drama rests on actions, it would seem wholly reasonable to apply the phrase to plays as well. But once again we must be careful not to over-simplify the principle. What we need to focus on in analyzing characters in plays is the nature of the relationship between their actions and their words, as the following example will demonstrate.

In *The Duchess of Malfi* by John Webster, Duke Ferdinand of Calabria takes vicious and protracted revenge on his sister, the Duchess of Malfi, for her secret marriage, revenge which ends in her murder. In this, he is assisted by one of the most complex villains in drama, Daniel de Bossola. Bossola acts initially with hard-headed cynicism in his role of spy, then with callous cruelty in putting the Duke's wishes into effect. When his sister is killed, however, the Duke immediately regrets his actions and turns on Bossola, who replies:

> Sir,
> I served your tyranny, and rather strove
> To satisfy yourself than all the world,
> And though I loathed the evil, yet I loved
> You that did counsel it; and rather sought
> To appear a true servant than an honest man. (4. 2. 308-14)

Now, while in drama it is action that reveals character, as it is in life, it is also the case that two different people may carry out the same action for different motives. Here, Bossola is not simply making excuses. His claim, however, is misleading. He has carried out the Duke's orders in a wholly calculating way in order to obtain social and financial advancement, not out of any 'love' for his master. Even so, there is some truth in the claim that he "loathed the evil". This side of him is revealed earlier when he praises Antonio's virtues to the Duchess, not knowing that Antonio is her secret husband. His praise is evidently sincere, not a stratagem to discover the truth – although this is the way it works out, for it encourages her to tell him of her marriage. This raises the question of how a man who not only recognizes virtue in another, but clearly *values it in that other* too, can act so viciously himself. The mere ambition for self-advancement is not a sufficient answer.

Bossola is defined as a character who suffers from *melancholy*. The modern term for this is 'depression,' but there is a significant difference between the early seventeenth century understanding of melancholy and the modern idea of depression. Bossola is energetic and alert, but his mood is 'black'. He is quick-witted and speaks his mind freely, to his social superiors too. He adopts a role that has much in common with the Fool or Jester (as does that other great melancholic character of the period, Hamlet,) to point out the folly and vanity of the world, but humourlessly. His view of life is bleakly cynical, as summed up in the lines:

> Of what is 't fools make such vain keeping?
> Sin their conception, their birth weeping,
> Their life a general mist of error,
> Their death a hideous storm of terror. (4. 2. 167-170)

And yet, on another level, this is a kind of mask, not one worn to disguise him to the world but to disguise him to himself, for he is running away from his own idealism. He becomes able to commit such evil only insofar as he hides his 'better nature' from himself.

The complexity of a character like Bossola is not something that can be inferred from his actions alone. What he says matters too. In good drama, however, speech is a kind of action (a point that will be developed later).

Moreover, Bossola's complexity is set off by the contrast with Duke Ferdinand. The latter is wholly defined by his actions – the actions largely carried out on his behalf by Bossola. He is not simple either, but his complexity is of a very different kind, more the 'complexity' of a psychopath. Whereas Bossola 'masks' himself to himself, the Duke is truly blind to himself and seems to have no idea at all of his own true motivation in taking such inordinate revenge on his sister. At one point he claims that he did not want her to marry so that he, or his family, would inherit her estate on her death. He also complains that she has married a social inferior. Neither 'reason' remotely approaches an explanation of the perverse cruelty which leads him to have wax models made of the 'corpses' of her husband and children, in order to persuade her that they have all been killed, and then to surround her with lunatics. In fact, the only plausible explanation of such sustained and uncontrollable rage is jealousy caused by a strong but suppressed incestuous desire. Nonetheless, although the Duke's words do not reveal his true motivation, they are revealing of his character in other ways, especially in their spitefulness and irrationality.

Sometimes, however, the principle that actions speak louder than words holds true in plays in a quite straightforward way. In Vaclav Havel's one-act play *Protest*, set in Czechoslovakia under Communism, a successful and relatively affluent TV producer called Stanek invites an old associate, a political dissident and human rights activist called Vanek, to his home to try to persuade the latter to organize a protest on behalf of a recently imprisoned pop singer, Javurek. Stanek's primary motive is that his daughter is pregnant by Javurek, although he claims – and no doubt believes – that he would also like to make a more principled stand against the totalitarian system for the sake of his peace of mind and self-respect. Vanek, it turns out, has already organized just such a protest and asks Stanek to sign the petition. At this point Stanek begins a very long monologue in which he 'thinks aloud' about the 'objective' and 'subjective' pros and cons of such an action. He is aware, of course, that it would be the end of his TV career and middle class life style (Vanek himself is only recently out of prison and impoverished), as well as having negative consequences for his children's opportunities in life, but asserts that all this would probably be worth it when set against the subjective benefits of living according to his conscience and principles. However, when he considers whether or not his signature would actually benefit the cause of Javurek's release, as the objective dimension of the decision, he comes to the conclusion that the opposite would be the case, since the very importance of a new name such as his among the dissidents would cause the authorities to harden rather than soften their stance. Hence he decides that for objective reasons he will not sign, although for subjective reasons he would certainly like to do so.

Throughout the play, Vanek says very little. Once the decision is reached, he does not try to change Stanek's mind. As a political dissident, Vanek is a man of action. We do not exactly witness this in the play, but, knowing it, we see that his relationship to words is quite the opposite of Stanek's. Stanek's long monologue in particular is disingenuous, a rationalization of his inaction. He is really trying to persuade Vanek by means of *words alone* to see him as he would appear were he to take the *action* of signing the petition.

> **WRITING EXERCISE:**
> **THE POWER OF SILENCE**
>
> Write a short scene for three characters in which one character does not speak. The speechless character must not be mute by reason of physical disability, unconsciousness or any device such as a gag, but by free choice. There is a conflict between what the two speaking characters want and what the mute character wants. However, situations such as interrogation and torture should be avoided. It may well be that the speaking characters want something which they believe to be best for the other character. In the conflict which arises, the silence of the one character effectively forces the other two to keep talking, although they have the option of talking to each other as well. Who wins?

ACTIONS AND ACTIVITIES

Stanislavski makes a useful distinction between two different ways in which characters in plays 'do things,' calling the one 'actions' and the other 'activities'. Given that a character usually wants to achieve something and that the situation s/he is in poses some kind of obstacle to achieving it, an action is what the character does in order to overcome that obstacle. An activity, on the other hand, is more or less everything else the character does in the course of her or his life as seen on stage. In Beckett's *Waiting for Godot,* for example, both Vladimir and Estragon want Godot to 'save' them, which basically means to take over responsibility for their lives. The obstacle they have to overcome is the absence of Godot. They try to overcome this by *waiting* for him, and waiting is their *only* action. Everything they do to pass the time while waiting is a mere activity.

The actions which truly speak louder than words are actions as strictly defined here. Activities, on the other hand, will often not speak louder than words, for they may be routine or relatively trivial, but they may yet be revealing of character in some cases. By definition they are not aimed at achieving what the character really wants, for if they were they would be actions instead, but they are not random and they may help define what kind of person a character is. When, for example, Hedda Gabler plays with her pistols at the beginning of Act Two, it constitutes an activity that is very revealing. It shows the reckless, irresponsible side of her character, as well as her 'male identification'.

Sometimes, what a character does is an activity on one level but an action on another level. Stanislavski's own example of this is Act 3, Scene 4 of *Macbeth*, where Lady Macbeth's activity is to host the banquet but her action is to cover up for her husband's distraught state of mind.

Harold Pinter makes especially effective use of a kind of blending of action and activity. In Act Two of *The Caretaker*, Davies, the tramp, returns to find that the light won't switch on. Mick then begins vacuum cleaning the flat in complete darkness (he has plugged the vacuum cleaner into the light socket). Terrified, for he does not know who is there, Davies takes out his knife. When Mick re-fits the bulb and the light comes on, he casually explains to the knife-wielding tramp how his brother and he take it in turns to do some "spring cleaning". Here, Mick's activity is "spring cleaning," however odd it is to do this in darkness, while his action is the (deliberate) intimidation of Davies.

Small-scale activities such as serving coffee are known as 'business' in the theatre. Pinter commonly turns business into action too. For example, in Act One of *Old Times*, Kate simply stands and goes to a table to take a cigarette. But the way she does this interrupts, fully intentionally, a conversation about her between Deeley and Anna. The pause this creates before her verbal intervention puts her in a position of relatively greater power.

SPEECH AS ACTION

If they are asked 'What is the main function of language?' many people will answer 'Communication'. But this is very questionable. Communication is certainly one function of language, but probably less important than either *social bonding* (which is what much conversation is for) or *getting what we want*. Of course, we may try to get what we want by openly communicating our desires. But we may also try to get what we want more indirectly, even manipulatively. In fact the biologist Richard Dawkins once suggested that all animal communication systems are systems for manipulation, human language among them. Although this may challenge our sense of our special status as a species, one need only think of how a young child tries to get round its parents or how a politician tries to persuade the public that a war is 'morally correct' to see the truth of the suggestion.

If it is true that people use language to get what they want in life, it is all the more true in drama. This is the other side of the coin of the maxim that 'actions speak louder than words'. When we see words being used to try to affect the outside world in some way (an outside world that contains other people), then we see that speech is another form of action. This is true even of Stanek's long rationalizing monologue in *Protest*, which was discussed above. Through it, Stanek is trying to persuade Vanek to believe that he, Stanek, is truly a dissident at heart who must unfortunately sacrifice his principles for rigorous objective considerations. Why should he want to do this? Basically, it is to help him believe it himself.

A dramatist may make very strong use of the principle that speech is action, as Aeschylus does in *Agamemnon*. When Agamemnon returns from Troy, his wife Clytemnestra welcomes him with a brazen speech. Not only is it shocking – or rather, it *would have been* shocking to a fifth century Athenian audience – for a woman to make a speech in public like this, but in it she emphasizes her own bitter suffering during Agamemnon's ten-year absence. In effect, this speech humiliates the returning hero, both in the way it is about the 'wrong things' and in the way it is spoken by the 'wrong person.' Not only is it as much a part of Clytemnestra's revenge as her subsequent murder of him, but it is also the part of her revenge that the audience actually witnesses.

While not all cases are as obvious as this, it often helps to ask, 'What effect is this speech intended to have on the listeners?' The answer may be straightforward, where the speech expresses a rational demand, or it may be more obscure. When, feeling betrayed by Ophelia, Hamlet tells her, "Get thee to a nunnery" (3.1), what does he really want her to feel – and to understand?

Where the answer to a question like this is not explicit in the words spoken, it must be found in the *subtext*.

SUBTEXT

In reading dialogue in plays, we sometimes need to distinguish between *what the words say* and *what the character really means* as s/he speaks these words.

Imagine two characters, A and B, who have just had a big row. They have now fallen silent. After a few moments, A asks: 'Are you still mad at me?' B replies: 'No'. But the abrupt, rather aggressive way she says this implies the opposite. Thus B can *say* 'No' but *mean* 'Yes'.

Certain exercises for actors are based on this distinction, but take it to an extreme. For example, an actor is given a line which is neutral in itself, such as "Can I make you a cup of tea, or would you prefer coffee?" S/he is then asked to speak this line to someone else as though it really means any one of the following: a) 'I find you the most boring person in the world'; or b) 'I really want to go to bed with you now'; or c) 'I don't think life is worth living any longer, so please help me'; or d) 'don't be angry with me, but I've got a confession to make'.

Still, in many real-life situations, the underlying meaning – the *subtext* – of an utterance is not entirely disconnected and different from what the words themselves say, but an extension of it. Consider the 'simple' line, "I love you". Assume also that it is spoken honestly. The statement is certainly not *just* the communication of information: 'it happens to be the case that I love you'. Most likely, it is also asking for something; "I love you" means 'I want something from you'… maybe your body, maybe your soul, maybe I just want you to say "I love you too" because I've had a bad day and I'm feeling insecure, or I want you to stop being angry with me, or cold towards me… and so on. The three words spoken are just the tip of an iceberg.

In drama, what the submerged part of the iceberg is, of course, has to be inferred from other things within the play-text, from other more explicit speeches, perhaps, or from character as this is revealed through action, or from the exigencies of the situation. Well-written plays are those that make this possible – though they do not necessarily make it easy.

It helps to realize that what a character *really means* is what that character is *really trying to communicate*. Subtext, thus, does not involve 'covering something up'. It is not like lying or trying to deceive another. On the contrary, it is quite open – in a certain sense. But it is also indirect. Hence the question always arises, why is the intended meaning not made fully explicit in the words spoken? Of course, there is not a single answer to this question, for it depends on the given circumstances. A person may say "I love you" to mean "forgive me" because they are too proud to ask forgiveness directly, or because they are manipulative, or because they do not really think they have done wrong but want the issue buried anyway… and so on. A person who says "No" (I am not angry with you) but means "Yes" (I am angry with you) may be *trying not to be angry*, but so far unsuccessfully, or may be trying to avoid setting the argument off again, or may be trying to communicate 'Yes, I am still angry with you, but I consider it pointless expressing that fact to *you*'!

Very broadly, we can distinguish two different kinds of subtext. In the first kind, characters mean more than they say because the situation they are in is itself 'deeper' or more complex than either they want to express openly or are able to express verbally. We can call this evasive subtext, though the degree to which evasion is willful is variable. In the second kind, characters deliberately and consciously imply something more or other than they say. We can call this manipulative subtext.

Examples of evasive subtext abound in Eugene O'Neill's *Long Day's Journey Into Night*. Dialogue in the early stages of this play is dominated by something that remains unspoken, Mary's drug addiction. This is unspoken both because it is too painful and too shameful to acknowledge, but also because of some strange, irrational, almost 'magical' belief that Mary can only overcome it if it is 'forgotten' – which of course it never can be. Yet the principle proposed above that subtext is trying to communicate something rather than 'covering it up' remains true. While the characters avoid explicit and open reference to Mary's addiction they are in fact referring to it and even, in a sense, 'discussing' it on a different level, because they *need* to.

The plays of Chekhov too are rich in this kind of subtext, though not in a way that suggests 'seismic forces' at work under the surface, as is the case in O'Neill. Nor are the characters necessarily trying to evade something, though sometimes – as, for example, in *The Cherry Orchard* – some of them are. The inability of so many of Chekhov's characters to express themselves fully is more an index of their failure to 'live fully,' a failure that they also typically fail to understand. The essential 'paradox' of Chekhov's drama, however, is that this 'failure to express' is itself very expressive! In *Three Sisters*, for example, Irena's and Toozenbach's last dialogue before his duel says so much in the way it leaves so much unsaid.

The second kind of subtext, manipulative subtext, is common in the plays of Harold Pinter, to the extent that it is like a 'key' to his work. Pinter's characters typically give the sense not that they are leaving something that *might be said* unsaid, but that they have some kind of *ulterior motive* for saying what they say. To put this differently, a speech is like a move in a game. This implies that, for Pinter, the principle that speech is action is strong. Indeed, in a play like *Old Times* there is little non-verbal action. Conversely, all speeches are actions. As a corollary of this, very little that the characters say can be trusted as a source of hard information. But if speeches are 'moves in a game,' the game is very serious and played in earnest. It appears as a 'game,' then, because there is nothing substantive, such as wealth or political power or fame, to be won or lost. Instead, the mere fact of winning or losing is what matters, as it is for young children when they play 'snakes and ladders'. At the same time, one of the 'rules' of the game is that it must not be acknowledged to be a game!

In this play, the game proceeds by characters making claims or assertions about what happened in the past. It is not permitted to others to deny or even to question these claims. But they can adopt them as part of their own versions of the past, changing them somewhat in the process. For example, Deeley tells the story of how he first met Kate. He saw her sitting *alone* in an otherwise empty run-down cinema, in a seedy suburb, watching a film tellingly called *Odd Man Out*, then 'made a pick up' outside. Later, Anna casually mentions having gone with Kate to such a cinema to see the same film, where they were *almost alone*. In this way, she 'takes over' Deeley's story but implies that she was there too. Deeley's move had excluded Anna (making her the 'odd man out'). Her move cancels this, and even seems to imply that no 'pick up' could have occurred. Deeley is obliged to accept this. But he does not respond to it. Instead, he changes the subject.

WRITING EXERCISE:
THE UNSPOKEN

This rather difficult writing exercise is closely related to the devising exercise called 'Breakfast Time' given earlier in this chapter, but tries to shift some clues as to the subtext (which is of the 'evasive' kind) into the dialogue itself.

Write a scene in which two characters are talking about some subject while one of them wants to confess or express something much more important but difficult to talk about to the other, and therefore tries to steer or lead the conversation round to a suitable 'opening'. However, when this is achieved s/he thinks better of it and says nothing. Can you do this so that the audience becomes aware not just that one of the characters has something to say but also of what this is, while leaving the other character credibly unaware of it?

WRITING EXERCISE: 'I'VE HAD ENOUGH!'

Imagine two people in a close personal relationship who have been arguing. One says, "I've had enough!" The other responds, "*I've* had enough!" The first increases the volume, "I've had *enough*!!" The other throws the same line back….

There are many acting or devising exercises in which the same word or line is repeated over and over by two participants, varying the expression, intonation and emphasis, but in such a way that (even if the phrase is nonsense) some kind of dramatic coherence and continuity is projected. This requires that each variation is a genuine response to the immediately preceding one.

Can you *write* such a scene, for two – or perhaps three – characters? To do so, you will need to choose your one line carefully. It should be such that it can be used to mean or suggest more than it says. You will also need to define the situation precisely. Non-verbal action, indicated by stage directions, can play a big part in this. But above all you will need to know what each character is trying *to achieve* with the line each time s/he says it, for this is an exercise in suggesting 'manipulative subtext'.

DRAMATIC EQUALITY

In a novel, the narrative voice is usually a *controlling voice*. This does not necessarily mean that the narrator speaks on behalf of the author, nor even that the narrator is reliable, but that the narration is the principal means of telling the story with other non-narrative means, such as dialogue or direct thought, being framed by it.

Plays do not have a 'controlling voice' in this way. Any narration made by a 'messenger' is framed by and contained within the dramatic action. In plays, even story-tellers, who are able to speak directly to the audience, must 'drop out of sight' for significant periods, leaving the action to 'speak for itself'.

Sometimes, however, a specific character seems to speak on behalf of the author. This may be very obvious. The Maniac in Dario Fo's *Accidental Death of an Anarchist,* for example, is a character with much in common with a traditional Fool or Jester, whose antics serve to expose and 'deconstruct' the corrupt and reactionary state apparatus of the police. Towards the end of the play we learn that this has been entirely deliberate. The Maniac turns out to be an anarchist himself who is able to articulate political truths on behalf of Fo.

Accidental Death of an Anarchist is a comedy, a hilarious political farce. It is more difficult for a character to speak on behalf of the author in a drama. Or rather, a particular condition must first be met: not *all* the other characters can be fools! That is to say, there must be some kind of worthy opponent of the character who carries the 'truth' of the play.

Nora, in Ibsen's *A Doll's House*, certainly embodies in her actions and (up to a point which is consistent with her character) articulates Ibsen's own point of view. To put this differently, Ibsen's intention is to demonstrate dramatically that Nora's choice of action in leaving her husband is not just defensible but entirely justified. To be a 'worthy opponent' to her, her husband, Torvald, does *not* need to be seen as having a valid or credible point of view about what kind of institution marriage is and what the duties of a wife are. But his character must be constructed in such a way that *an actor can portray him sympathetically.* No such need arises in a comedy such as *Accidental Death of an Anarchist*. On the contrary, the actors who play the various policeman are invited to 'send them up' as fools (but note that the best way to do this is to play these parts 'straight,' for the policemen themselves do not know they are fools).

The point can be seen even more clearly in relation to Strindberg's *The Father.* In this play, the Captain embodies and articulates many of the playwright's own beliefs, while the Captain's wife, Laura, embodies much that he detested and held to be dangerous. Moreover, Strindberg thought of the theatre as a 'weapon' with which to combat the advance of feminism and undo the damage done to the interests of the male sex by the likes of Ibsen! Nonetheless, as a true dramatist he had to create in the character of Laura a part that allows the actress to 'play it from the inside'. The actress, that is, is able to ask, 'What would I do in such circumstances, if I were Laura?' – where 'if I were Laura' means 'if I had the same goal as Laura'. Insofar as such a question can be *sincerely* asked, the actress will be able to find a way of playing the part that does not seek in any way to draw the audience's attention to what is 'wrong' with Laura.

How is the 'dramatic equality' of a character like Laura evident in the text? This is a difficult question to answer without a much more detailed analysis than can be given here. In broad terms, we are made to feel that there is 'more to' the character than that side of her which is expressed in her conflict with her husband. We can imagine her in other situations, not involving conflict. Hence she is not reducible to the Captain's opponent. This is certainly not true of the police in Fo's play. As characters, there is nothing more to them than the fact that they are policemen.

Of course, many plays have no character who embodies or articulates the dramatist's own viewpoint. But if these are dramas involving external conflict, they too need 'dramatic equality' between their principal characters. This need not be a perfect balance of forces. A football match between a very strong side and a very weak one may not be perfectly balanced, but *so long as it is not fixed* it is still a match between 'equals'. Exactly the same applies to drama.

CHARACTERS IN COMEDY

Characters in comedy are often types with little psychological complexity. Very broadly, we can distinguish two main kinds: firstly, those who embody some kind of *social* role or characteristic, such as the strict father, or gossip, or pedantic doctor; secondly, those who embody some of the intrinsically comic nature or spirit of the buffoon or jester or clown.

Characters of the second kind can seem to have a kind of independent existence beyond the specific play. This is especially true in the very important tradition of Commedia dell'Arte (in which plays were improvised rather than scripted), but only to a lesser extent in the later scripted plays that were based on this tradition, such of those of Goldoni, Moliere and more recently Dario Fo. In true Commedia dell'Arte, the basic characters are always the same, no matter what the play. These characters were often associated with a particular half-mask and, in a particular troupe, were always played by the same specialized actors. Certain characters came to have an existence independent of the specific story and, especially in the case of roles such as Harlequin (Arlecchino), the performer himself was visible in many of the routines, antics and even acrobatics that made up part of the entertainment. In a case like this, the 'character' exists as it were 'half-way between' the fictional story and the real performer, exactly as does Charlie Chaplin's Little Tramp. This can never be so true of the scripted plays that count as literature, but up to a point we are made to feel that a role such as that of the Maniac in Fo's *Accidental Death of an Anarchist* has a kind of independent existence (in other words, that he might appear in another, different play) and that the 'theatricality' of this role involves a kind of self-conscious display of performance itself. Thus the Maniac embodies that 'anarchic' feature of Commedia in which the *Zanni* (comic servants) were able to disrupt and temporarily 'derail' the main action.

QUESTIONS TO ASK ABOUT YOUR SET PLAYS

1. **Does the play contain any characters who stand outside the dramatic action? If so, what is their role in the play?**
2. **Which characters are proactive and which are reactive? Do any reactive characters function as confidants?**
3. **Which characters, if any, change or develop through the course of the play, and why?**
4. **Are there different kinds or 'levels' of secondary characters? What functions do secondary characters have?**
5. **Are certain characters confronted by choices in the plot? How important are such choices in the development of the plot and in establishing character?**
6. **What is the objective of a given character in a specific scene?**
7. **What is the super-objective of a given character in the play as a whole?**
8. **What actions does the character perform in order to achieve either his/her objective or his/her super-objective?**
9. **How do such actions reveal character?**
10. **Does a given character perform any activities (as against actions) that serve to reveal character?**
11. **In certain key scenes, does a given character 'say what s/he means and mean what s/he says' or is there a significant distinction to be made between what a character says and what s/he means?**

12. How much of a given character's thoughts, desires, motives etc. has the playwright put into speech and how much has to be inferred? Either way, is this to be explained in terms of the nature of the character or in terms of the style of the play?
13. How does a given character use speech (as distinct from other kinds of action) to get what s/he wants?
14. Does any character seem to embody the 'truth' of the play, either in their actions or in their words or both? That is, is there a character who embodies or articulates the playwright's own point of view? If so, how do we know this? Above all, has the playwright opposed such a character with a worthy adversary? If not, does it matter?
15. If there is external conflict in the play, is it a 'match between equals'?

CHAPTER THREE
DRAMATIC STRUCTURE

In general, the *structure* of a play – or of a novel or a poem – can be defined as the *interconnectedness of its parts*. But what are the 'parts' of a play?

Separating the different parts of a play from each other is not as straightforward as separating the different parts of an automobile engine. A play may be divided into three acts, with the curtain rising at the beginning and falling at the end of each, or it may be divided into many shorter scenes with just a brief blackout between one scene and the next. In these cases the parts – the acts or scenes – are obvious, and formally distinguished from each other. But suppose we want to divide the action into a 'beginning, a middle and an end'. In this case it may not be so clear where the beginning ends or the end begins. This suggests that we can use the word 'parts' to mean different things. More fully, in drama there are different kinds of parts existing on different levels of the play's structure.

The most basic level of structure is the through-line of actions which constitutes the 'backbone' of the play. If we list the key actions of a play in sequence, then each action can be thought of as an essential part of the play as a whole.

Division of the action into scenes or acts is a way of 'framing' these key actions, sometimes separately (where the play is divided into short scenes) and sometimes as groups of actions in sequence (where the play is divided into longer acts).

SCENES AND ACTS

We can define a scene change as a change of time and/or place and say that whenever there is a change of time and/or place, then the scene changes. The first scene of Shakespeare's *Hamlet*, for example, takes place on the castle battlements at night. The second scene takes place inside the castle, possibly in the throne room, the next morning. Such scene changes are marked in the text, of course, but an audience in the theatre will obviously also understand that the scene has changed without any actor having to announce "Scene 2".

But this is not the only way in which plays are divided. Play texts from the French, Italian and Spanish tradition commonly mark scene changes whenever any character either enters or exits. In such cases the action may well remain continuous, that is, without any change of time and/or place. It may be thought, then, that this kind of division into scenes is a convention of play texts alone and has little relevance when considering plays in performance or even as intended for performance. Up to a point this is true, but it should not be forgotten that in well written drama the entrances and exits of characters are always significant moments, and that an entrance or an exit changes the dynamics of a scene in such a way that there is a kind of 'action change,' if not a scene change in the other sense of the term. In general in reading plays, it is a good idea to pay close attention to the effects on the action of entrances and exits.

Now, texts of Shakespeare's plays are divided into five acts as well as into usually smaller scenes, but an audience in the theatre is unlikely to notice a change of act in the same way that it will notice a change of scene. We shall turn to the question of why this 'higher level' division into acts is made at a later stage. First, it is necessary to note that in many plays which are divided into acts, an act is really a long scene. When the act changes, that is, there is a change of time and/or place, but during the act there is no such change. But while this kind of act is really a scene, that is, a segment of the play's action which is continuous in time and confined to one location, there is a major difference between a short scene and a very long one.

Shakespeare tends to fit the structure to the action rather than fitting the action to the structure. That is, he changes scene whenever the action requires it. If there is no need to change time and/or place, then a scene can be very long; Act 5 of *Measure for Measure,* for example, is a single scene, as is Act 5 of *Twelfth Night*. If the action consists of a battle, on the other hand, he often uses a quick succession of very short scenes, each involving individual skirmishes, in order to build up the bigger picture. His plays, in fact, are quite similar to movies in the way they 'cut' from scene to scene as and when the action requires. But changing scene in a play is not quite so simple as changing scene in a film.

The Shakespearean stage was an 'empty space'[1] – almost no set and very few props were used. Instead, the imagination of the audience, stimulated by the heightened, poetic language of the play, was required to fill in the setting. This feature, of course, allowed quick scene changes, since there was no scenery to shift. In addition to this, Shakespeare very often begins a scene *in medias res* – a phrase which means 'in the middle of things'. This device allows, for example, two characters to enter in the midst of a conversation, even as other characters are exiting, thus diverting the audience's attention from the potential awkwardness or 'flatness' of the exit and maximizing the smoothness of the transition.

In performing those modern plays which are structured in many short scenes, it is common to use the device of a brief blackout during a scene change. A blackout – which obviously should not last too long – allows actors to go off and come on, and even allows some minimal change of set to take place, all unseen by the audience. But a blackout is not simply a convenient practical device, for it also has some effect on the way scenes are experienced by the audience. A blackout tends to add strong emphasis to the last line or gesture or action of a scene, as though the whole scene leads to that crucial last moment, which is what the audience is expected to retain of it in memory. Modern dramatists who write this kind of play very often structure their scenes with this effect in mind, so that the last speech or image is clearly where they want the emphasis to fall. Shakespeare does not write his scenes this way.

The kind of emphasis or 'underlining' achieved by a blackout at the end of a short scene is not typically climactic. In act-based drama, on the other hand, a sequence of events throughout an act usually leads to some kind of climax, or at least to a significant turning point in the plot

---

[1] The title of a very influential book about the theatre: Peter Brook's *The Empty Space*, first published in 1968.

as a whole. This moment in the action is sometimes called a 'curtain' because it immediately precedes – and in a sense makes possible – the fall or closing of the curtain. It is a moment in the plot which is so significant that it may even allow the actors to freeze in a *tableau* for the duration of the closing of the curtain. An 'effective curtain' is one which satisfies the audience that the act is 'complete' and (except in a play's final act, of course) makes them keen to see what happens next, especially if an interval follows. (Note that at the end of an act, a sudden blackout would seem too abrupt – unless it were to follow a relatively prolonged freeze. A fade-out, on the other hand, works in exactly the same way as the closing of a curtain.)

Straightforward examples of 'effective curtains' occur in Henrik Ibsen's *Ghosts*. At the end of Act One, Mrs Alving and Pastor Manders overhear Osvald attempting to embrace and kiss the maid, Regina, in the dining room. This deeply disturbs Mrs Alving since it 'replays' something she has just confessed to Manders, that her own husband had seduced a maid many years earlier. Manders even deduces that Regina is the illegitimate daughter of the late Mr Alving. The curtain falls as Mrs Alving has to take Pastor Manders' arm in order to steady herself and walk towards the dining room. The end of Act Two is more 'crudely' or obviously climactic: a fire breaks out at the Orphanage, causing all the characters to run out. Of course, where a climax *should* be, there an anti-climax *can* be. Samuel Beckett's *Waiting for Godot* is structured in two acts. At the end of each, the news arrives that Mr Godot cannot come that day. In each case, Vladimir and Estragon decide to leave, then do not move. This inversion of conventional structure perfectly fits a play that can be described as an anti-drama.

CLIMACTIC AND EPISODIC STRUCTURE

The two kinds of dramatic structure called 'climactic' and 'episodic' are commonly discussed together because in many ways they are opposites. Although we should not to assume that therefore *all* drama tends to be either climactic or episodic (or even somewhere 'in between'), a great deal of world drama can be usefully analyzed in these terms.

In episodic structure there are usually relatively many episodes, each of which tends to be relatively 'self-contained'. These episodes are usually connected together in an over-arching plot, but – at least in truly or fully episodic structure – this plot is not where the main significance of the drama lies; instead, it is simply a means whereby the separate and successive episodes are 'tied together'. Note, then, that episodic structure requires relatively many short scenes. It is not likely to be act-based.

Climactic structure, in contrast, is likely to be act-based. In climactic structure the plot is much more tightly organized than in episodic structure and can even be described as having a certain definite 'shape'. This shape is called 'Freytag's pyramid'. The metaphor of a pyramid suggests that the action 'rises' in some way, then 'falls'. There is thus an upward slope and a downward slope. At the top, there is a climax – hence the term 'climactic'.

Metaphors, however, can be dangerous – at least a little misleading. A useful metaphor should imply a valid analogy of some kind. Notice then that the 'rising action' usually creates a rather longer upward slope than the downward slope that follows the climax, for if the latter were equal in length the play might end in prolonged tedium. Hence we can only visualize a lop-sided pyramid. Perhaps, then, we should leave visualization behind and ask, what is it that really 'rises'? That is, what is the valid analogy embedded in the metaphor?

When we speak of 'rising expectations' or 'rising tension' or 'rising prices,' the idea is that something is increasing. In the so-called 'rising action' of a drama, what is it that increases? There is not a single answer to this question: it may be the pressure on the protagonist, or her or his knowledge of the difficulty of a situation; it may be the complications of the plot; or it may be the feeling of tension or suspense in the audience. Of course, it may well be some combination of these.

The climax is a point at which this increase ceases, but for a good reason. For example, the reason may be that the pressure on the protagonist becomes so great that s/he is forced to act in some drastic way, thereby solving a problem; possibly it is that the hero makes an important discovery, causing a major change in the way s/he acts. The basic rule is that *at the climax, something changes.*

In Sophocles' *Oedipus the King,* the rising action is Oedipus' gradual discovery of the truth. The climax of the action is where he finally learns that he has killed his father and married his mother. At this point, he exits into the palace, where he blinds himself. This action itself can be thought of as climactic in relation to the story, but the audience learns of it indirectly, through the report of a messenger. The play's 'falling action' follows, where, firstly, Oedipus explains to the chorus why he blinded himself (the chorus already knows his story, of course, since it was present at the discovery, but it still finds his subsequent self-mutilation excessive) and, secondly, he gradually finds the courage to impose on himself the sentence he had pronounced much earlier on the murderer of King Laios – exile.

Now, the falling action of a play leads to or includes its *resolution* or *denouement*, terms that imply that something is solved or unravelled. However, we must be careful not to apply them unthinkingly.

Something is solved in *Oedipus*, of course – the mystery of the killing of Laios – but this is climactic, not part of a resolution of the action. Oedipus' act of self-blinding is a 'resolution' of sorts, since it is an act of atonement, and the same is true of his departure into exile. But precisely because Oedipus himself feels that the whole of this exile, that is, the rest of his life, is required to atone for his life up till now, it seems strange to claim that anything is 'resolved' here, at least in the usual sense of the term. Dramatically, the 'resolution' is best thought of as the last part of the play following Creon's entrance, since the latter has to 'press' Oedipus to carry out his sentence of exile on himself. Moreover, here Creon represents the future of Thebes as its new ruler.

Aristotle claimed, in the *Poetics*, that the tragic plot involves a *reversal of fortune*. It is clear that Oedipus goes from good to bad fortune and that he does so precisely at the climax of the play, at the moment of his discovery of the horrible truth. We can say in this case then that what changes at the climax is Oedipus' fortune.

The basic concept of Freytag's pyramid is useful so long as it is applied flexibly and not unthinkingly mapped onto the actual formal divisions of the play. Freytag himself based the idea on an analysis of five-act structure, such as that found in Elizabethan plays, but it may well be simplistic to identify the five phases of the action – exposition, complication, climax, falling action or reversals, and denouement or catastrophe – with the five acts. In any case, many plays are not divided into five acts, but into two, three or four.

> ## 'THREE ACT STRUCTURE'
> The relatively common concept of 'three act structure' is a useful simplification of Freytag's pyramid. The three 'acts' in this case are *exposition, complication* and *resolution*. However, this structure need not correspond exactly to the actual or formal division of the action into acts, if there is one. (Note that the concept is often applied to movies, where no such division is made.) Moreover, a single act, or even a single short scene, can embody its own 'three act structure'. Clearly, there is some relation between this concept and the commonplace distinction between the beginning, the middle and the end (see below). It also corresponds to the Japanese concept of *jo-ha-kyu*, which Zeami, writing of the art of Noh Theatre, said was the basic principle of both dramatic action and structure. According to this principle, everything dynamic has a three-part 'shape' in which energy is expressed and directed in different ways, beginning with some kind of preparation, followed by some kind of development, and ending with something like 'braking'. Not only the action as a whole, but each segment of it, and each component action within each segment, must follow the 'law' of *jo-ha-kyu*.

In Ibsen's three-act *Ghosts*, there is a climax at the end of Act Two, the burning down of the orphanage, which is 'bigger' than that required for a curtain, and this feature corresponds to pyramidal structure. Moreover, Act Three begins with what appears like falling action, for the characters, or rather most of them, assume that the worst has happened, that the 'tragedy' has already taken place. But very soon new complications appear and the action begins to rise again (a device that is not uncommon in drama). The true climax of this play comes right at the very end. Following this, however, there is no 'falling action' at all, no resolution of any kind, no denouement. Mrs Alving is left in a situation in which her son, Osvald, has sunk into madness, and she must decide whether to kill him, as he has previously asked of her, or to let him live. If she kills him, she will have to live with the guilt of this act; if she does not, she will have to live through his slow and pitiful disintegration as a human being – a choice of evils if ever there was one. The curtain falls before she decides.

Until this point, Mrs Alving has continued to believe that she has positive choices, in other words that there is hope. At each point where she tries to act positively, events take a different turn and her hopes are dashed. Her situation becomes increasingly difficult, but before the end of the play it is never desperate. With each turn of events she learns more of the truth and believes that this allows her to take better control of the situation. But what she learns at the very end is that she has no control over events whatsoever, although with terrible irony it is still she who must not only act, but who must chose the act.

The end of *Ghosts* is disturbing. It is as though Ibsen intended the audience to be left with a 'bad feeling' caused by the play's lack of resolution. In fact, the end of this play has something in common with the so-called 'in-yer face' drama of later twentieth century British writers such as Edward Bond. It confronts – and leaves – the audience with a problem, as if to say 'this is what your values lead to, so *you* resolve it; don't expect the playwright to do that for you'!

Ibsen's four-act *Hedda Gabler* is less abrasive and confrontational in its implicit attitude towards its audience, but it still ends abruptly with Hedda's suicide. Here too, the audience is left to make sense of events for itself. In this case, however, a very subtle distinction can be made. Suicide is a resolution for Hedda herself (and the true climax of the drama can be located at the end of Act Three, when Hedda burns Loevborg's manuscript), but nothing is resolved for the other characters who are simply left in shock. The question, then, is whether the audience in the theatre is 'with Hedda,' having come to understand and sympathize with her, or 'with the other characters'. If the former, the play will end satisfyingly (albeit unhappily) with a sense of resolution, but if the latter, it will leave the audience with a kind of problem, rather like *Ghosts*.

Certain kinds of comedy also embody climactic structure, but use it to different ends. In such cases, the rising action usually consists of complications of the plot, leading to a climax that may well be some kind of impasse. Commonly, the resolution which follows depends on some fortuitous, often highly unlikely, turn of events. Oscar Wilde's *The Importance of Being Earnest* exhibits all these features. The impasse arises because Lady Bracknell will not give her consent to the marriage of her daughter, Gwendolen, to Jack Worthing, for the reason that he does not know who his parents were, while Jack will not consent to the marriage of his ward, Cecily, to Lady Bracknell's nephew, Algernon, until she does so. All is resolved when it is discovered that Cecily's governess was in the employ of Lady Bracknell twenty-eight years previously. At that time, in a "moment of mental abstraction," Miss Prism had lost a baby by mistakenly placing it in a handbag, which had been left at Victoria Station, having placed the manuscript of her three-volume novel in the baby's pram instead. Since Jack had been found in a handbag at Victoria Station, he is now discovered to be Algernon's older brother and Lady Bracknell's nephew.

Even a play that violates the normal logic of cause and effect can exhibit some kind of 'rising action' leading to a climax. In Ionesco's 'anti-play,' *The Bald Soprano,* the action 'builds' primarily through the device of increasing the number of characters on stage, from two to four (when the Martins join the Smiths) and then to five (with the arrival of the Fire Chief). The 'climax' of this play immediately follows the exit of the Fire Chief when all remaining sense and logic is lost and a very animated conversation consisting of increasingly nonsensical non-sequiturs becomes a shouting – or screaming – match between the four remaining characters. There is, however, nothing that corresponds to 'falling action'. Instead, the screaming abruptly stops and the play begins again, but with the Martins having replaced the Smiths. The existence of something like climactic structure in this case suggests that this play is a parody of conventional theatre. To this end, it violates *one* principle of dramatic construction, Aristotle's precept that the action should be 'probable or necessary'. This one violation is all the more starkly seen because the play retains the kind of shape it would have had had the principle been respected instead!

> Earlier, it was noted that Shakespeare's plays are divided into acts as well as into scenes. The question arises of whether this 'higher level' division has significance and, if so, what? This is a difficult question. Of the playwrights of the period, only Ben Jonson is known to have tried to structure his plays according to 'classical rules,' which included the Roman writer Horace's recommendation of division of the action into five acts. However, it was two actors, John Heminges and Henry Condell, who first divided the texts of most of Shakespeare's plays into five acts in preparing the First Folio edition seven years after the author's death in 1623, thereby 'elevating'

> their cultural status by implying a classical model. Still, such a division would not have been imposed entirely arbitrarily, but based as far as possible on major shifts in the nature of the action. But it is obvious from the diversity of Shakespeare's dramatic output that he did not write according to prescribed rules, so we must ask of each play independently whether the division into acts is worth taking any account of or not.

'FATE'

Insofar as climactic structure leads to a climax, then one of its key features is *tight plotting*. This means that the events which make up the dramatic action are closely connected to each other in a sequence of cause and effect, as need not be the case in episodic structure. One thing leads to another with a kind of inevitability. More than this, the stories of plays with strong climactic structure very often extend back into the past, so that events which took place in the past have significant knock-on effects into the present. We saw earlier that this is the case with both *Oedipus* and *Ghosts*. Indeed, this feature is one reason for the feeling of 'inevitability' in the plots of such plays. The present has already been determined by the past.

The past also matters, in a very different kind of way, in *The Importance of Being Earnest*. But here the effect is just the opposite. Nothing is inevitable. Instead, everything is coincidental. Such a comedy certainly does not make us feel that there are benevolent powers watching over us. The very contrivance of the plot, in fact, is self-parodying and pleasure arises *because* the resolution is all 'too good to be true'.

The feeling of inevitability in the action, in drama as against comedy, is easy enough to associate with the idea of 'fate'. Oedipus was in fact fated to kill his father and marry his mother. Ironically, whatever he did to try to avoid his fate brought him closer to fulfilling it. In this sense, Oedipus' actions were not 'free'. They were determined. However, everything Oedipus does during the course of the play, he does freely. His efforts to find out the truth and his act of self-blinding are not fated at all, but the result of an exercise of free will. (The way Sophocles makes the chorus question whether Oedipus' self-blinding was necessary underscores this.) But this fact does not dispel the sense of inevitability that attaches to the dramatic action, a sense that consists in the following: given what has happened in the past, and *given that Oedipus is the kind of man he is*, then the outcome of the play cannot be otherwise.

It is the same in *Ghosts*. 'Fate' in Ibsen's play is not decided by the gods, but by a virus. Osvald, that is, has inherited his father's syphilis. This will destroy him no matter what anyone does. But more subtly than this, Mrs Alving determined the outcome of events for herself when, many years earlier, on the advice of Pastor Manders, she put social duty above emotional need and returned to live with her dissolute husband. Through the play, she continues to believe that she can somehow disassociate herself from that action – by using her late husband's money to found an orphanage so that she herself does not remain indebted, by telling Manders the truth about her husband's depravity, and so on. Earlier, she had tried to protect Osvald both by sending him away to school and by preserving his good image of his father. In short, as a character Mrs Alving is very largely defined by her belief that she can control the situation created in part by her own decision to be a 'good wife,' if only in various damage limitation exercises. Events show that she cannot. Worse, they show this to Mrs Alving herself.

THE BRECHTIAN CONCEPT OF 'EPIC THEATRE'

It was precisely the feature of *apparent* inevitability that led the German marxist playwright Bertolt Brecht to reject what he called 'Aristotelian' or 'dramatic' theatre (which can largely be associated with climactic structure) and to develop his own kind of 'epic theatre' (which is episodic in structure) instead. Brecht argued that 'dramatic' theatre causes the audience to be carried away by the flow of events, often making them sit on the edge of their seats with anticipation or suspense. This, he claimed, prevents the audience from *thinking* about what they are witnessing; it privileges emotional involvement over dispassionate reflection.

Epic theatre is a theatre of 'interruptions'. Made up of short scenes, each scene change is an interruption to the action which should provide the audience with a 'thinking space'. The focus is no longer on where the action is leading, but on what has just been witnessed. (Of course, Brecht used other devices, both as a writer and as a director, to encourage the audience to react critically. See Chapter Four for a discussion of his so-called 'alienation effects'). A consequence of this approach is that each scene is constructed as a small-scale play in itself, or 'playlet,' with its own distinct structure and purpose. While it remains true that the scenes are linked together in a plot, so that the play as a whole tells a coherent story, the content and shape of each separate scene is not wholly or primarily determined by the needs of that plot; instead, the scene is primarily determined by the point it exists to make or to draw attention to. For this reason, at the end of a scene there should be no suspense or anticipation, although naturally we remain interested in how the story turns out.

Epic theatre, being episodic in structure, tends to tell *different kinds* of stories than are told in climactic structure. Since an epic play can cover a long period of fictional time, there is no need to relegate earlier parts of the story to the past. In climactic structure and where the past is determinative, a significant part of the present action necessarily involves the discovery or reassessment of the past. This implies some kind of learning process for at least one character. But this is not necessary in epic theatre, although of course it is possible. For Brecht, the most important feature of epic theatre lies in this: it replaces the way in which *characters* learn through experience with the way *audiences* can learn through witnessing.

ONE UNITY OR THREE?

In about 330 BCE, the Greek philosopher Aristotle wrote an important treatise on the nature of tragedy, called the *Poetics*. Not only is this a valuable source of information about ancient Greek tragedy itself (although Aristotle wrote a hundred years after Sophocles and Euripides were at their height), it is also in many ways a wise and insightful account of serious drama in general.

THE SIGNIFICANCE OF ARISTOTLE'S TITLE, *POETICS*

For many centuries the principal medium of drama was verse. Although Elizabethan plays contain some prose sections, often but not always those involving 'low life' characters, plays were not written entirely in prose until the end of the nineteenth century (apart from some seventeenth and eighteenth century comedies). Ancient Greek tragedy was composed entirely in verse. But the title *Poetics*, and the many references to 'poetry' and the 'poet' within the work, have very little to do with this fact. In Greek,

> 'poet' is *poiitis*, which literally means 'maker'. In fact, the English 'playwright' is a strict translation of *poiitis* in the context of drama, since 'wright' (from the Old English *wyrcan* – to work) literally means a maker. Aristotle's main concern is with the way the 'poet' shapes the action of tragedies, in other words with dramatic structure.

Much later, sixteenth century Italian scholars proclaimed the doctrine of the 'three unities,' claiming the authority of the *Poetics* as their origin. The three unities are the unity of *time*, the unity of *place* and the unity of *action*. The principle of the unity of time, most strictly interpreted, states that the action of a play should occupy the same amount of real time as it takes to perform this action on stage. Aristotle, however, says nothing of the kind. He notes in passing that Greek tragedians often restricted the time of the action to 'a single circuit of the sun' (and the principle is often more loosely interpreted as requiring just this), but he does not argue that this is what should be done. The principle of the unity of place states that all the action of a play must take place in a single location. Aristotle does not mention this at all. However, he does insist on the unity of action.

Before we consider what the principle of the unity of action is, we should note that the doctrine of the three unities was very influential. Sixteenth and seventeenth century dramatists in Italy and France adhered to these rules, strict as they are, in writing tragedies in particular. This discipline, in the work of a playwright such as Racine, gives the drama great intensity and compression. Rather than the often surprising twists and turns of a play by Shakespeare, who had a total disregard of the unities of time and place (which were known in England at the time, and approved of by court writers such as Sir Philip Sidney), a tragedy by Racine steadily and unrelentingly builds a sense of inevitable catastrophe. (Note also that plays which observe the unities of time and place are very likely to be dramatizations of the climactic last parts of much longer stories, like Sophocles' *Oedipus the King* and Racine's *Phèdre*.)

According to Aristotle, the principle of the unity of action basically means that a play should tell *one* story, not more than one. He criticizes writers who suppose, for example, that 'because Heracles was one man, the story of Heracles must be one story'. The 'life story' of a particular individual is made up of many, loosely related stories. Instead, the test of whether a story is one story or not is much stricter; it should be the case that if any of the incidents which are included in it is either removed from it or moved to a different place within it, the story as a whole will be 'broken' and lose coherence. Put differently, every incident in the story must not only be necessary, but must necessarily occur in its own proper place in the sequence of incidents.

This condition can only be met if incidents are all related one to another in a causal sequence, so that removal or relocation of any incident would beak the chain of cause and effect. On this basis Aristotle argues that the events of a tragedy must be 'probable or necessary'. What makes a particular event probable or necessary is not just the preceding events, but also the character of the person or persons involved in it. The question to ask of any action is whether or not this action is what this kind of person would do in these or similar circumstances. Hence an aspect of the unity of action is *consistency of character*.

A circularity can arise in relation to the last point. Only if we already know what kind of person a character is can we ask if an action is consistent. But in plays, character is revealed through action. In one sense, then, character is necessarily consistent with the action which reveals it! However, Aristotle's point holds in relation to the play as a whole, in that although characters may change or grow, their actions at the end of the play should be consistent *on some level* with their actions at the beginning. Now, this phrase 'on some level' is important for a modern audience, since the modern understanding of human psychology allows characters to appear as consistent to us who would have been inconsistent to Aristotle.

For the student of drama, the concept of the unity of action is a useful analytical tool rather than a test of whether or not a play is good. In other words, it should not be applied prescriptively, but as one means of distinguishing plays from one another. Some plays, that is, observe the unity of action but others do not. Climactic structure is more likely to have unity of action than episodic structure, but this should not be taken as a strict equation. Some climactic plays lack it, at least in a strict interpretation, while some episodic plays have it.

CASE STUDY: PLACING A SOLILOQUY

We can ask of any event or action within a play whether it is necessary or not, and whether it occurs necessarily where it does. Sometimes this question leads us into deep water. Consider Hamlet's famous soliloquy, meditating on suicide, which begins:

> To be, or not to be, that is the question –
> Whether 'tis nobler in the mind to suffer
> The slings and arrows of outrageous fortune,
> Or to take arms against a sea of troubles,
> And by opposing end them. To die, to sleep….

It seems clear enough that if this soliloquy were cut, the plot of *Hamlet* would remain the same, in the sense that all subsequent events would be unchanged. Yet *Hamlet* without this soliloquy is unthinkable. Without it, we would know less of Hamlet's thoughts and feelings, and in that sense less of his character. Insofar as it reveals something about him, it belongs to 'Hamlet's story,' but it does not belong to the sequence of cause and effect which leads from the first appearance of the Ghost to the deaths of most of the principal characters, including Hamlet himself. (To 'force it' to belong to this sequence, we would have to argue that, in this soliloquy, Hamlet chooses to go on living, if only for the negative reason that what comes after death is unknown. Had he chosen suicide instead, subsequent events would certainly have been different!)

What of the placing of the soliloquy in the sequence of events? As a matter of fact, there is evidence that Shakespeare tried placing it at different points in the play before finally settling on Act 3, Scene 1. This is too complex and technical a matter of textual scholarship to go into here, but it is quite obvious that the soliloquy can be placed differently, precisely because it does not belong to the sequence of cause and effect of the plot. But this is not to say that its actual placing makes no difference. On the contrary, wherever it is placed it will be understood by the audience as belonging to another kind of sequence, the sequence of Hamlet's states of mind, and this too needs to make sense.

Act 3, Scene 1, however, is probably the most surprising place that Shakespeare could have chosen. At the beginning of the play Hamlet is severely depressed, ostensibly because of the hasty remarriage of his mother, Gertrude, to Claudius, Hamlet's uncle, following his father's death, and he expresses the wish to die in the soliloquy, "O that this too too solid flesh would melt…" (1. 2. 129ff). He then learns from his father's Ghost that he, Hamlet's father, had been murdered by Claudius. Hamlet swears to take revenge. But a supernatural apparition is not necessarily "honest" and may even be a malicious spirit in disguise. Hamlet therefore delays. At the end of Act 2, some players arrive to perform in the castle. Hamlet realizes that he can test the Ghost's story by having the players perform the story of just such a murder. The watching Claudius will then betray his guilt – if indeed he is guilty. Act 2 ends with the famous lines, "The play's the thing / Wherein I'll catch the conscience of a king." Here, Hamlet's mood is entirely positive and 'upbeat'. This is not just because he has found a potential way out of a metaphysical impasse, but also because he loves theatre. He is evidently happy that the players are here and because he can involve himself in their preparations, quite apart from 'catching' the king's conscience.

On his very next appearance, a mere fifty-six lines into Act 3, Hamlet speaks the "To be, or not to be" soliloquy. This is shocking. The soliloquy appears 'unmotivated,' that is, we do not know what triggered this new bout of melancholy. To reach for a modern psychological explanation, for example that Hamlet is 'bi-polar,' does not help, for it fails to explain the *dramatic impact* of the soliloquy. Instead, we need to note that this soliloquy is very different in tone from the earlier "O that this too too solid flesh would melt". The earlier soliloquy is an emotional outburst. This one is a dry, intellectual meditation. It seems that Hamlet has replaced one metaphysical impasse (the question of whether or not the Ghost is "honest") with another (the 'unknowabilty' of what lies after death). Moreover, this new difficulty is expressed in an extraordinary way. We cannot know what comes after death because death is an "undiscovered country from whose bourn / No traveller returns". Then what of the Ghost? Is the Ghost not a traveller returning from that undiscovered country (temporarily, of course)? Although Shakespeare was tolerant of minor inconsistencies in his plays, being well aware that an audience in the theatre would not spot them, this seems to be a deliberately placed 'inconsistency'. It gives us the impression that, in his philosophical meditation, Hamlet has entirely forgotten about the Ghost!

To understand this more fully – and to see how it relates to the unity of action – we need to go a step further. For Aristotle, a character should act in the way that that 'kind of person' would act in the given circumstances. Today, we also hold that action in plays is an expression of character. Moreover, actions make up the plot. But *Hamlet* differs from the general rule in an important respect. Hamlet is required by the Ghost to carry out an action, the action of taking revenge on Claudius. Hamlet's story, then, becomes the story of his relationship to this 'contractual duty'. He is *bound* to carry out this action, but at the same time it is not really 'his' action; it is the Ghost's, in the sense that it expresses the Ghost's desire. Hamlet thus becomes the Ghost's agent. But that can never be *all* that he is. This clearly complicates the question of what actions are 'consistent with' or 'express' Hamlet's true character. It is also why, at the end of the play, the dying Hamlet insists that his friend, Horatio, live on, though Horatio wants to join Hamlet in death, in order to "tell [his, that is Hamlet's] story," for Hamlet is aware that 'his story is not his true story'. That is, if only the basic sequence of events is recounted, Hamlet will appear as a man who failed more than he succeeded in carrying out his duty, one whose procrastination caused, directly or indirectly, the deaths of so many along with the actual target of revenge, Claudius. But such an account does not tell us *who Hamlet is*. What Horatio is charged to do, then, is to tell the story of a man who was cast in a role which was not his own.

Now, while all this complicates our sense of the unity of action and the associated concept of the consistency of character, the important thing is that most people will feel that *Hamlet* has 'unity of action' after all. Moreover, though there may not be a 'necessary' place for the famous soliloquy, there is a best place for it – no doubt that which Shakespeare settled upon, in Act 3 Scene 1, where it most effectively 'disengages' Hamlet from the action of carrying out the Ghost's demand and even from the plot itself.

MAIN PLOTS AND SUB-PLOTS

One way in which plays can fail to have unity of action, at least in the strictest sense of this idea, is by incorporating a sub-plot. By definition, a sub-plot cannot be 'necessary,' since if it were, it would be part of the main plot. The unity of action requires that the play tell 'one story,' but a sub-plot implies a second story. At the same time, however, playwrights may *integrate* their sub-plots with their main plots in order to establish another kind of unity.

Sub-plots are relatively easier to include in episodic than in climactic structure. However, the other side of this coin is that episodic structure imposes less need to integrate the sub-plot with the main plot. In *The Tragical History of Doctor Faustus*, for example, Christopher Marlowe simply switches from main plot to comic sub-plot with scene changes.

Usually, a sub-plot is a plot with its own central character or characters, different from the central character or characters of the main plot. But plays do not normally tell two *entirely separate* stories at once. Hence either a main character in a sub-plot is a secondary character in the main plot (like Wagner in *Dr Faustus*), or some other character or characters link the two plots. In Ibsen's *Ghosts*, for example, the central character in the main plot is Mrs Alving herself, while the central character in the sub-plot is Engstrand. Regina and Pastor Manders have roles in both plots.

Ibsen tightly integrates the sub-plot with the main plot in this case by making the action of the former have an impact on the latter. The fire in the orphanage is Engstrand's doing, part of his scheme to put pressure on Manders, but it has the effect of undermining Mrs Alving's own project, at least in part. But in spite of such linking or 'overlapping' of the action, the sub-plot remains a sub-plot because it is driven by Engstrand's 'super-objective' (the opening of a profitable 'Home for sailors,' or brothel) where this is *not in conflict* with Mrs Alving's super-objective.

The most important question, of course, is: *why* do playwrights sometimes include sub-plots in their plays? There is, naturally, no single, all-purpose answer to this question. The sub-plot in *Ghosts* serves at least three purposes: it is a means of introducing complications to the main plot, it helps reveal more of the character – or rather the naivety – of Pastor Manders, and it provides, in the character of Engstrand, an image of true moral corruption against which Mrs Alving's apparent change of mind about her late husband makes better or fuller sense. Marlowe includes a sub-plot primarily to entertain his audience with some knockabout comedy and to a lesser extent in order to separate scenes in the main plot more fully from one another, but he also uses it for contrast; if Wagner and Robin can conjure devils, then magic is hardly the supreme form of learning that Faustus takes it to be. Contrast is a relatively common function of sub-plots, in fact (note that it is the third function of the sub-plot in *Ghosts*, as identified above), and it can be developed to great effect. In Shakespeare's *Twelfth Night*, the 'high romantic comedy' of the main plot is offset by the 'low comedy' of the sub-plot in a way that greatly enriches the play. Seen separately, the world of the high comedy would appear affected, indulgent and pretentious, while the world of the low comedy would seem crude and vulgar. Mixed together, the overall impression is of the complexity of human character and behaviour, something that cannot be reduced to a single set of conventions.

The example of *Twelfth Night* is instructive. It should make us ask, what is the cost of the unity of action? What, in other words, does the unity of action cause to be left out of the 'imitation of life' that is a play?

THE BEGINNING, THE MIDDLE, AND THE END

In the *Poetics*, Aristotle asserts that the action of a tragedy should have a beginning, a middle and an end. This may seem obvious, but in fact it is well worth saying, provided that it is properly understood. Aristotle is not referring to the fact that a performance – or for that matter, a reading – of a play will necessarily begin at some point in time and end at a different, later point in time. His assertion concerns the play's action and implies that this should be self-contained and should constitute a whole. Only if the action has a beginning, a middle and an end will we feel that it is complete. If we do not feel it to be complete, then we will not be satisfied by it.

The assertion is useful also because it implies that beginnings, middles and ends differ from each other in certain crucial respects. However, Aristotle develops this point only abstractly, saying that a beginning is naturally followed by something but preceded by nothing, a middle is naturally both preceded by something and followed by something, and an end is naturally preceded by something and followed by nothing. This is not very helpful.

There are really two problems here. The first concerns how we distinguish between beginnings, middles and ends. For a given play, this boils down to locating the 'end of the beginning' and the 'beginning of the end'. The second concerns the nature of the relationships that exist between the beginning, the middle and the end, for these relationships vary from play to play.

Christopher Marlowe's *The Tragical History of Doctor Faustus* tells the story of a scholar, Dr Faustus, who is granted magical powers for twenty-four years by Lucifer in return for his soul. It is very easy to distinguish the beginning and the end of the action of this play. The beginning comprises all the action through to and including Scene 5 in which Faustus signs away his soul. The end is simply Scene 13, the last scene of the play, in which Faustus' time runs out and he is taken to hell. The seven scenes in between are the play's middle. [1]

What makes the above distinctions so straightforward is the very nature of the story or plot of this play. Normally, events occur during the middle of the action of a play which affect its end. But here, Faustus' fate is sealed at the 'end of the beginning'. The actual end of the play, then, is simply the direct consequence of that beginning. It follows that the middle is nothing more than the separation in time of the end from the beginning. Although it covers twenty-four years, nothing of consequence happens during this middle part of the play. There is no plot development or complication, only disconnected and 'illustrative' episodes from Faustus' life (together with the sub-plot). For this reason, *Dr Faustus* is a 'broken backed' play. Structurally, that is, it is weak, although this reflects the very nature of its subject – a subject which has exercised a fascination for audiences whatever the weaknesses of the play.

Marlowe uses the middle as best he can to chart the degeneration of Faustus' character. As time goes by, Faustus' practice of magic becomes increasingly trivial and debased, ending in little more than practical jokes or attempts to escape *ennui*, although initially his

---

[1] This analysis refers to the 'A' text, not the longer 'B' text. The latter is an expanded version of the former, made after Marlowe's death, which reflects the play's popularity at the time.

desire was to understand the secrets of the universe and to use his power to grand or worthy ends. Moreover, the option of repentance remains, so that the middle part of the play is also the story of Faustus' failure to repent. But in spite of this, it remains the case that the middle of this play lacks real drama (though it is not short of theatrical effects). All real drama is in its beginning and its end.

It is useful here to try to imagine an alternative *Dr Faustus*. In this imaginary version, the whole action of the play would take place on the last day, or even the last evening, of Faustus' life. Instead of Marlowe's episodic structure, this version would be climactic. It would tell the story of Faustus' life, perhaps to a confidant, at least back to his decision to sign his soul to the Devil. Dramatized this way, the story would be 'the iceberg' and the plot 'its tip' (whereas story and plot coincide in Marlowe's play). Now, such a version need have no problematic middle, for it is the plot of a play rather than its story that should have a beginning, a middle and an end.

Having said this, we need to see that it complicates our understanding of beginnings. This is because the beginning of a play's action or plot may come in the middle of its story. The whole (beginning, middle and end) of Sophocles' *Oedipus the King* can be thought of as the *end* of Oedipus' story. Indeed, almost all plays assume some kind of past, even *Dr Faustus* (before this play begins, Faustus has become a renowned scholar and has become bored with all conventional learning). What, then, becomes of Aristotle's idea that a beginning is naturally followed by something but *preceded by nothing*?

Fairly obviously, this idea should not be taken too literally. Instead, we can say that where a play has a linear, chronological plot that involves some kind of transformation (as most do), the beginning is the part of the play in which the situation before the transformation is established, while the end is the part in which the situation after that transformation is established. At the beginning of *Oedipus the King*, to take a very clear example, Oedipus is at the height of his success. At the end, he is blind, morally shattered and about to go into exile. Although various events have led to the situation which is shown at the beginning of the play, none of these events need be seen by us for us to be able to understand the nature of that situation, and this is the sense in which 'nothing comes before' that beginning.

A play in which no transformation occurs, such as Beckett's *Waiting for Godot*, necessarily presents a problem here. If there is no transformation, how can the end differ from the beginning? And how can the middle differ from either the beginning or the end? Moreover, if there is no real difference between the beginning, the middle and the end, how can the action seem to be 'complete'? Of course, this lack of differentiation is, in large part, the point of the play. Yet Beckett cunningly 'solves' the problem (of 'completeness') in the very way he draws our attention to it. He does this by means of the characters of Pozzo and Lucky, who appear in each of the two acts of the play. In large part, it is because of Pozzo and Lucky that each *act* seems to have a middle, although we should not identify either of these middles with the precise time that they are onstage; rather, each act seems *in retrospect* to have had a middle. Now, this lends a sense of completeness to each act, which is satisfying enough, and it allows Beckett to strengthen the sense of parallelism between the two acts. This parallelism works in two ways. On the one hand, the structural repetition emphasizes that the play *as a whole* has no distinctive beginning, middle or end, in the sense that nothing develops or changes. On the other hand, the *parody of a transformation* in Pozzo and Lucky – in Act Two, Pozzo has become blind and Lucky has become dumb – draws our attention to the way in which time not only involves repetition, but also decline. Thus while Vladamir's and Estragon's situation does not change through the course of the play, Beckett manages to give to the action of the play a strong sense of completeness.

As a general rule, students of drama should pay close attention to the natures of the beginnings, middles and ends of plays they study. It should be clear from the discussion above that both the differentiation of these parts and the relationships between them are variable. It is necessary therefore to analyze each play in its own terms. But the concepts of the beginning, the middle and the end are always useful, no matter how experimental or unconventional the play.

Caryl Churchill's *Blue Heart* is made up of two one-act plays. In the first of these, *Heart's Desire*, the action begins with a father, Brian, and mother, Alice, waiting for their thirty-five year-old daughter, Susy, to arrive from the airport, for she has just flown in from Australia. Brian's sister, Maisie, waits with them. But the action never gets beyond the beginning. This is because every few moments or minutes, the action stops and is 'reset,' either to the very beginning or to some other prior point in it. The scene is then replayed as it was for a brief time, but it always turns out differently, sometimes very differently. In one scene, Maisie falls and injures herself; in another, we learn that a murder victim has been found in the family's garden; in another, Alice confesses to having been unfaithful; in another, a friend of Susy's arrives instead of Susy; in another, a ten-foot high bird arrives, and so on. In each case, these 'events' are erased in the next version of the beginning. Churchill pushes this to extremes. In one scene, gunmen burst in and kill the family. They are alive again, of course, in the new beginning that follows. The play then ends with what seems to be the actual arrival of Susy, followed immediately by a last 'new beginning' consisting of only the play's first line.

What is the effect of this violation of normal structure? Once the audience grasps the convention, the usual interest in 'what happens next' (that is, in a sequential plot) is replaced by an interest in 'what happens in the next version'. But this is no longer an interest in *how one thing leads to another*. Instead, each version presents an 'alternative universe' and this is something that can be enjoyed for its own sake, a kind of theatrical playfulness. Even so, many spectators will still try to spot some sort of development through the course of the play, perhaps even something analogous to 'rising action' through the succession of scenes. What they will find is a slow and fragmented establishment of what seems to be the 'true version' of events, and this is the scene as played at the end of the play, just before the final reset to the play's opening line. Nothing 'dramatic' happens in this version, but the tensions and hostilities between the three waiting people are revealed. In retrospect, the spectator may even come to the conclusion that all the 'deleted' events were symbolic extensions or fantasy enactments of these tensions and hostilities. But looked at another way, *Heart's Desire* may simply be an experiment with form and a way of 'teasing' the audience.

A play such as this does not *undermine* the dictum that dramatic action should have a beginning, a middle and an end. It is a one-off violation of the principle, which works only insofar as the device seems to be fresh and original. In other words, no other writer, after watching or reading this play, is going to think that here is a new way of structuring *plays* – as against this one play.

There is probably more scope for writers to vary the ways in which their plays end. We have already seen that the concepts of resolution and denouement are of variable relevance, even in climactic plays – for the climax can come very near the end or earlier. Broadly speaking, the ending of a play should be satisfying in some way and determines the audience's 'last impressions'.

In comedy (which is partly defined by its requirement of a happy ending), very contrived endings can be perfectly acceptable, even enjoyable because they are contrived, as in Wilde's *The Importance of Being Earnest*. But this is not always so. Moliere's *Tartuffe* resorts to a 'deus ex machina,' a messenger from the King who solves all problems and saves Orgon from Tartuffe. This is less satisfying, although to the play's original audience it would have been understood as flattering to the existing king, Louis XIV. Sometimes the 'contrivance' of the ending of a comedy can be unsatisfying not for aesthetic but for other reasons. Kate, in Shakespeare's *The Taming of the Shrew,* is a strong, independently-minded woman who must be made to submit to male authority. To a modern audience, Kate's final submission to Petruchio, especially her speech about the duties of a good wife, tends to be unconvincing and even undesirable. Today, many prefer to see this ending played in an ironic, hence insincere, way. The ending of Shakespeare's *Measure for Measure* is especially problematic. This strange, experimental 'problem play' is closest to a comedy of vice and folly, but Shakespeare inverts the traditional ending of such a comedy by letting his vicious character, Angelo, go free, and having the fool, Lucio, punished instead, while simultaneously substituting the 'obligatory' ending of a romantic comedy (which this play most definitely is not) – marriage all round!

In modern plays, the end sometimes involves a kind of 'return to square one'. This is true in a straightforward way of Churchill's *Heart's Desire*, of Beckett's *Waiting for Godot* and of Ionesco's *The Bald Soprano*. It is true in a more subtle way of Pinter's *Old Times*. This play comes to a climax when Kate – who throughout has been a laconic character – speaks a relatively long monologue which effectively 'wins' and so concludes the power struggle between the three characters, reducing Deeley and Anna to silence. What follows is very strange. In silence in fact in a kind of minimalistic, slow 'dumb show' – the three enact a scene. To make any sense of it, the audience must remember something said by Anna in Act One, a description of this very scene as something that had happened twenty years earlier. If this link is made, the three characters appear as trapped in some kind of endless cycle of repetition, and Kate's 'victory' becomes entirely hollow.

Why do many modern plays end like this? The question is far too big to answer properly here, since it involves a major cultural shift with deep historical roots. For our purposes, it is an aspect of the shift in the focus of drama from *plot* to *situation* that began with Chekhov. Crudely, a focus on plot is a focus on change and development, while a focus on situation is a focus on the absence of change and development.

TIME IN PLAYS

Drama is a linear art form, like music. A play only exists in time, unlike a painting or sculpture. Plays tell stories, moreover, which are also presumed to take place as linear, chronological sequences of events.

In this section we shall examine the different relationships that can exist between *stage time* – the time it takes to represent something on stage – and *fictional time* – the time it would take that same thing to happen in reality and hence the time that is presumed to pass in the story. We shall also examine how the chronology of the story itself is constructed.

In many plays, there is a perfect coincidence between stage time and fictional time: the time it takes to represent an action or scene on stage is exactly the amount of time it would take for this same action or scene to take place in reality. This is true of the episodes in Greek tragedy, for example, and of the naturalistic drama of the late nineteenth century. But note that during the choral odes or *stasima* that separate the episodes in Greek tragedy, a great deal of time can pass in the story while only a few minutes elapse in the performance.

A dramatist can play with the idea of time while not actually undermining the coincidence between stage time and fictional time. Ionesco does this in *The Bald Soprano* by frequently making the clock strike randomly different times at random intervals. While this device reflects the absurdity of the world of the play, nonetheless the action develops in chronological sequence and in a way that neither increases nor decreases the rate at which time seems to flow.

In Elizabethan and Jacobean theatre there is much greater flexibility or elasticity in the relationship between stage time and fictional time. Mostly, fictional time is compressed, which means that more fictional time passes than stage time. Shakespeare and his fellow dramatists realized that if, for the sake of experiencing a dramatic fiction, an audience is prepared to believe that an actor is a King and that a wooden stage is a battlefield, then it is also prepared to believe that a day can pass in a few minutes. A fine example is the first scene of *Hamlet*, where the Ghost appears at midnight and disappears just before dawn, a mere one hundred lines of verse later! A little less extreme, in the last scene of Marlowe's *Doctor Faustus*, the very last hour of Faustus' life – an hour which is precisely indicated by the striking of a clock – passes in forty-eight lines, which only requires between three and four minutes of stage time. Of course, this compression of fictional time is not a mere convenience; it greatly intensifies the dramatic power of the scene as Faustus awaits his damnation and fails for a last time to repent.

A play in performance lasts relatively little time, rarely more than three hours. The story it tells, however, commonly occupies days or weeks, sometimes even years. We have seen already that some plays enact only the last part of a longer story, in which case most of the time of the story is in the past. But the time of the story also passes between scenes. In this way, the story of Dr Faustus comes to take up twenty-four years, the amount of time allotted to him by Lucifer in exchange for his soul. In Shakespeare's *The Winter's Tale*, sixteen years elapse between the end of Act 3 and the beginning of Act 4, such a jump that it is announced to the audience by the figure of Time himself.

Mostly, however, dramatists respect what physicists call the 'arrow of time'. The drama starts at a certain point in the story, that is, and moves forward from there, without ever going backward. But there are exceptions. Some plays incorporate flashbacks. In Arthur Miller's *Death of a Salesman*, Willy Loman re-lives many memories which become so vividly real in his mind that they are enacted on stage as if they are happening here and now. Even so, the audience easily 'reads' this action as 'happening in Willy's head'. A more complex example is Harold Pinter's *Old Times*. Twice in the play, for no apparent reason, Kate and Anna (an old friend of Kate's whom she has not seen for twenty years) start talking as though they have been suddenly transported back twenty years and are living together again in a flat in London. Yet they clearly remain in Kate's and Deeley's house in the country, and Deeley himself clearly continues to exist in the present. The effect is mysterious (as, indeed, is the whole play) and not easily 'explained away' as happening in a character's mind.

In his play *Betrayal*, which is about marital infidelity, Pinter tells the story backwards. While the action of each scene is presented normally, the audience has to realize that in the story, Scene 2 comes before Scene 1, Scene 2 come before Scene 3, and so on. This device reflects the way in which it is common to try to explain (or excuse) behaviour such as infidelity by *referring back* to earlier events which led to it. In certain situations, in fact, such as criminal trials, it is 'natural' to tell stories backwards, since the object is to *retrace* rather than *repeat* the causal sequence. As we move backwards through the story, we are able to reassess what we have just seen in the light of new information about what happened before it. In a related way, in *Top Girls*, Caryl Churchill places all the scenes in chronological order except the last one. The action represented in the last scene takes place one year before the start of the play. This device forces the audience to reinterpret the story it has seen in the light of the new information it receives. (Recall also that the action of Churchill's *Heart's Desire* keeps rewinding and starting again, for reasons discussed above.)

An extreme example of departure from strict or normal chronology is Vaclav Havel's *The Increased Difficulty of Concentration.* The action of this play is not formally divided into separate scenes (such as are distinguished from each other in a text), but simply into two acts. However, when a character enters or exits, very often a shift in time – either forwards or backwards – occurs. This is facilitated by the specified set, which has four doors. A character may exit through one of these and almost immediately re-enter through another, differently dressed, at some other point in time in the story. Using various clues which have been carefully written into the play, the audience is required to sort out the puzzle and to piece the actual story (which all takes place in one day) together.

Why does Havel adopt such a device? To answer this, we need first to note that the play has three plot-lines which evolve in parallel, each involving the central character Huml. None of these is a main-plot, nor can any be called a sub-plot; they are of equal importance. The 'scrambling' of normal chronology mixes, or 'intercuts,' these different plots together in a way that would not occur if the action were ordered in temporal sequence. Moreover, Havel very often changes scene, jumping backwards or forwards in time and usually switching from one plot to another, in the middle of what would be a continuous segment of action in one of the plots if presented conventionally. The device emphasizes the equality of the different plots and reflects Huml's difficulty in organizing and integrating the different sides of his life, especially as this involves relationships with different women. Moreover, the device challenges or undermines something in the logic of conventional scene changes. For a scene to change in the conventional way, something in the action *must be completed*. But Havel's scene changes mostly occur before anything in the action is completed in this sense, leaving the action temporarily suspended. This too reflects the difficulty Huml has in balancing both his different desires and the different demands on him.

ANTI-STRUCTURE?

Rules, it might be argued, are there to be broken – at least in the case of the arts. This is only true, however, if the result is artistically worthwhile. More precisely, if the 'rules' – or better, the basic principles – of dramatic construction embody certain assumptions, assumptions not only about drama, but also about human life and about what is significant to human beings, and if these assumptions seem no longer valid, then and only then are the rules 'there to be broken'.

In *The Card Index*, Tadeusz Rozewicz consciously and deliberately violates nearly every assumption we have about what a play is. The play is set in a room which is simultaneously a street, with strangers passing through it. The central character, identified as 'Hero,' is at times a child, at times a young man and at times a middle-aged man, randomly, depending on how other characters treat him. He is called by many different names, even by a single character, and may well have different identities, or change identity as play goes on. He does nothing, or almost nothing. When the chorus of three old men complains about the lack of action, the Hero responds that he is scratching his head and looking at a wall, and asks if that is not enough. True, just after this he does murder the chorus, cutting off one of their heads, because they are preventing him from sleeping. But later they return to life. The other characters that appear are never expected. Sometimes they assume a relationship with the Hero. Sometimes they do not. Sometimes they just talk nonsense. The play itself is divided into two 'acts,' but in such a way that the audience might not realize it and might be left sitting in the auditorium for five or ten minutes waiting for the Hero to return. At the end, no curtain falls and no lights are extinguished. It might not be 'the end'.

The Card Index has no unity of action. It has no exposition, no complication, no climax, no resolution. It has no beginning, middle and end, except in a perfectly literal sense. It has no consistency of character, no consistency of location and no consistency of time, although in another sense location and time remain the same throughout. It does, however, have a point and a meaning. The world presented on the stage may *make no sense*, but it *makes sense that it makes no sense*. We understand, that is, that we are not watching anything unfold and develop because *everything has already happened*. At the end of the play, a journalist interviews the Hero only to learn that he has no significant hopes or plans for the future, no significant political views, no intention of doing anything to save the world or himself, both because it is only five o'clock in the morning and because it is *too late*. The disaster has already happened.

The disaster that has already happened is the Second World War, in particular the terrible sufferings of the Polish people during it. Realizing that spiritual and cultural certainties had been annihilated along with cities and people, Rozewicz believed it necessary to 'reinvent' theatre. The primary task of this new theatre for 'our great age' is to reflect truly and fully the collapse of all the old certainties. Does this make it purely pessimistic? No – for insofar as it succeeds in this, it is itself the first step in a reconstruction.

QUESTIONS TO ASK ABOUT YOUR SET PLAYS

1. What are the key actions that constitute the play's plot?
2. Is the structure of the play episodic or climactic?
3. Is it divided into scenes or acts or both? If both, why are the act divisions made where they are?
4. Does the location of the action change? How many different locations are there?
5. How much time passes between scenes or acts?
6. Do acts before the last one end with a 'curtain' or mini-climax? How is this achieved?
7. Why do shorter scenes end where they do? Is it simply to move on with the plot or is there any implicit emphasis on the last words or action of the scene?
8. Do shorter scenes have a purpose beyond their contribution to the development of the plot?
9. What is the beginning, what is the middle and what is the end? Where does the beginning end and where does the end begin? Are there different possible answers to these questions?
10. Between the beginning and the end, what, if anything, changes?
11. What makes the end satisfying – if it is? If it is not satisfying, why is this?
12. What, if any, complications of the plot occur and where?
13. What kind of climax, if any, does the plot come to?
14. Is there any resolution or denouement?
15. Is there unity of action? Is the plot such that no incident can be removed from it or moved to a new place in it without loss of coherence?
16. Is there a sub-plot? If so, how is it connected to the main plot and what is its purpose?
17. What is the relation between stage time and fictional time?
18. Is the action presented in linear chronological sequence? If not, why not?

CHAPTER FOUR
THEATRICAL MEANS AND ENDS

In the Introduction, the following definition was given: whatever seems 'theatrical' in a play is an aspect or quality of certain ways in which the *means of theatre* are used to present the fiction. In this chapter, we shall explore more fully how playwrights make use of the 'means of theatre' in order to achieve the effects they want.

First, however, note that the term 'theatrical' is sometimes used in relation to real-life situations, often in a derogatory way. If a person's behaviour is described as 'theatrical,' the implication is probably that it is excessive or exaggerated, and to that extent false. In more recent years, the same idea has come to be expressed in a different phrase, 'over the top' – sometimes just 'O.T.T.' – which also originates in the theatre. Now, there is something peculiar about the fact that theatre's own self-defining term, 'theatrical,' has acquired such a negative sense. After all, terms like 'musical' or 'poetic' or 'sculptural' have not done so. The reason for it is simply that performance in the theatre can easily become exaggerated, with performers 'over-acting'. Hamlet's speech to the players clearly indicates that this kind of over-playing was common enough in Shakespeare's time:

> Speak the speech I pray you as I pronounced it to you, trippingly on the tongue; but if you mouth it as many of our players do, I had as lief the town-crier spoke my lines.... Suit the action to the word, the word to the action, with this special observance, that you o'erstep not the modesty of nature. For anything so o'erdone is from the purpose of playing, whose end both at the first and now, was and is, to hold as 'twere the mirror up to nature. (3. 2. 1-3 and 15-19)

Moreover, when, towards the end of the nineteenth century, a new more naturalistic style of acting was developed by Stanislavski and others, the grand gestures and declamatory delivery of the earlier histrionic style came to be regarded with amusement as out-moded. Theatre, it was believed, should look more 'like life'.

Reactions against this somewhat restrictive attitude began early in the twentieth century, but nowhere involved any desire to return to the old style of acting. Even so, the 'rehabilitation of theatricality' – in other words the realization that theatricality, at least in some of its forms, could be a 'good thing' – did not really take hold until the 1960s. The reason it did so was the emergence of television drama as a competitor. TV drama is capable of giving at least the superficial impression of reality much more effectively than theatre. In response to its rapid growth both in quality and quantity, many of those working in the theatre realized that it was a mistake to try to compete with TV drama on *its* terms. Instead, the theatre should do what the theatre does best. Above all, it should make maximum use of the fact that it is *live*, that actors and audience share the same space or ground. In no way does this imply that theatre should return to 'over-playing'. What it does mean is that theatre should stop trying to *hide its own means* in the way it achieves its ends.

> ### A THOUGHT EXPERIMENT
> Imagine going to see a play, with which you are not familiar, in a language you do not understand. In one of its scenes, a character begins to behave in what seems to be a very emotional way, with strongly emphatic gestures and highly charged vocal tones. It occurs to you that either a) this is true characterization, which conforms to the way the play and hence the character have been written, or b) the actor is performing too 'theatrically' and quite possibly spoiling the performance for those who understand the play. How, if at all, can *you* tell the difference? If you come to the conclusion that you cannot, why is this?

The history outlined above is of course far more complex than such a brief sketch can do justice to. What matters here is simply the following. Theatricality is either positive or negative. Only its positive forms are relevant to the study of drama as literature, and then only if they are written into the play text.

Since theatricality arises in what might be called the 'visibility' of the means of theatre, it will help to review what these means are. They are the playing space itself, the actors, their costumes, the objects that make up the set, stage properties (called 'props'), lights, music and sound.

SPACE

For the student of plays in text form, space is easy to overlook. While the playing space is never a neutral element in a production, its relevance to the study of drama as literature depends on the play and above all on the way the playwright has written it. Does it seem that the playwright has written the play while imagining the fictional scene, that is, the supposed location or setting of the action, or has s/he written it while imagining the playing space and how this can be used instead? If the latter, at least if this is apparent from the text, then it is more likely that understanding the use of space is relevant to understanding the play.

A playing space is a real space, but it is also imaginary (it is part of the building the actors and audience occupy and part of the 'world of the play'). It can be transformed in imagination in a way that is aided by the set and lighting or simply by what the actors do. An actor can mime throwing a ball to a fellow actor a mere four metres away and the latter can mime catching it in such a way that the distance between the two of them appears like fifty metres. Or two actors can mime a boxing match or dancing a waltz while at a distance of several metres, but as though they are in close physical contact. For reasons complexly related to this, if a character has to walk a 'long (but straight) distance,' an actor can often achieve this on stage by walking in something like a semi-circle.

In some plays, this 'transformability' (in imagination) of the playing space allows a *change of location without a change of scene*. Earlier, in Chapter Three, a scene change was defined as a change of time and/or place. But in Act Four of the ancient Sanskrit drama, *The

Recognition of Sakuntala, by Kalidasa, a journey takes place on stage. Sakuntala and others leave the hermitage, heading for King Dusyanta's palace, and arrive at a lake. They enact the journey in two phases, in each of which they simply walk around the stage. As they do so, the audience understands that the location changes. In the second phase of their journey, it is also clear that time is compressed – they travel, that is, a relatively 'long way'.

Such 'low-tech' devices invite and rely on the imaginative participation of the audience, something which tends to be true of most if not all kinds of positive theatricality. Perhaps the most famous, because explicit, appeal to the audience's imagination to help in the transformation of the space is the Prologue that opens Shakespeare's *Henry V*:

> O for a Muse of fire, that would ascend
> The brightest heaven of invention,
> A kingdom for a stage, princes to act
> And monarchs to behold the swelling scene!
>
> ….
>
> But pardon, and gentles all,
> The flat unraised spirits that have dared
> On this unworthy scaffold to bring forth
> So great an object: can this cockpit hold
> The vasty fields of France? or may we cram
> Within this wooden O the very casques
> That did affright the air at Agincourt?
> O, pardon! since a crooked figure may
> Attest in little place a million;
> And let us, ciphers to this great accompt,
> On your imaginary forces work….

Yet, rather than *openly celebrating* the imaginary nature of theatrical spectacle, this sounds an 'apologetic' note – the "scaffold" of the stage is "unworthy" and the actors themselves are mere "ciphers" compared with the original participants in the story to be told. This is a 'trick,' of course, a means to sell the play to come, by underlining the greatness of its theme, rather than to belittle it, so that the prologue functions much like a trailer to a movie. Nonetheless, it still defines what might be called the 'essential triangle' of theatricality, a relation between three things: 1) the subject, theme or story, 2) the means of theatre (sketched here in a way that prefigures the concept of 'poor theatre'), and 3) the imagination of the audience.

In the case of some plays that are difficult to stage, it may help to know something about particular successful or simply innovative productions of them. Oscar Wilde's *Salome*, for example, specifies an upstage "cistern" from which the voice of John the Baptist is occasionally heard. It also includes the famous dance of the seven veils, followed by Salome's gruesome act of kissing the Baptist's severed head, which she carries on a silver platter. The 1988 London production directed by Steven Berkoff opted to engage the imagination of the audience in relation to all three problems. Firstly, the Baptist sat throughout in a painted dark square, inviting the audience to imagine the dark underground cistern. The fact that he was fully visible also increased the power

> of his presence, as this is felt by the other characters. Secondly, Salome removed no garments in her dance. Not only did this avoid any cheap titillation of the audience, but it also focused attention on the role of *Herod's* imagination in the eroticism of the scene. Thirdly, no prop was used for the severed head. Instead, Salome herself created it in the way she 'saw' it and reacted to it. Arguably, this approach to the play came much closer to realizing its poetic intensity and even Wilde's intention than any more crudely 'realistic' staging would have done.

SETS

Use of the playing space and use of a stage *set* to represent the fictional setting are closely related. Plays vary greatly in the kinds of set they require. As a general rule, episodic plays have simple, minimal sets, or no sets at all, for the practical reason that frequent scene changes need to be made. Act-based climactic plays, on the other hand, can make use of 'full' sets, although they do not have to. The fall of a curtain at the end of a relatively lengthy and dramatically satisfying act allows enough time for a major change of set, even if no interval occurs.

> Where the set is minimal or non-existent and the audience must imagine the location, the question arises of whether the actual stage space coincides with the whole of that location of the scene or just part of it. If the setting is external, the heath in *King Lear* for example, it will be the latter. But if it is some kind of room, it may be either. In Webster's *The Duchess of Malfi*, one character commonly exits immediately before another enters. Is this 'coincidence' (straining credibility)? Not necessarily, for if the imaginary interior setting is conceived as extending beyond the actual playing area, then the onstage characters see others coming before they enter. By convention, however, the character who is about to enter typically does not see one who is about to depart!

Sets also vary in the degree to which they are intended to appear as 'realistic'. At one extreme, in a 'box set,' the back and sides of the stage may well be screened with wall-papered flats, complete with painted portraits, windows and doors; the floor too may be carpeted, and the resulting 'room' fully furnished. At the other extreme, a relatively small amount of industrial scaffolding and nothing else may be used to represent all the parts of a castle. In the former case, nothing is left to the imagination of the audience. In the latter case, almost everything is. But in imagining the parts of the castle, the audience will be helped by the way the actors *use* the set.

A good rule of thumb in staging plays is that nothing should be put on stage which is not actually used (and used significantly in advancing the action rather than used casually) by the actors. Why then do some playwrights specify the kind of full set, usually a fully furnished room, where quite clearly it is impossible for the actors to use all its component parts, at least in a significant way? To put this question differently, why do such playwrights either fail to understand that the audience is capable of 'filling in' the setting in imagination or, what is more likely, actually seek to 'shut down' this imaginative capacity? These questions relate to an important but problematic phase in the history of theatre, which will be dealt with in the next section.

Between the extremes of 'full' and minimal sets, various possibilities arise. The set of Arthur Miller's *Death of a Salesman* is in one way 'full,' for it represents a house with kitchen and bedroom showing through 'transparent' (non-existent) walls, which are placed in line with the theatre's proscenium arch. These rooms are furnished and other features of the house are represented, though not to the point of perfect naturalism. Miller further specifies that an apron stage be used to represent the back yard of the house. But this 'back yard' is left entirely bare. The reason for this is that the apron is used also for all scenes in the past, or rather in Willy Loman's memory and imagination. Different conventions apply to these scenes. Whereas in the present action the actors never cross the imaginary line of the house wall, they are able to do so in the scenes that take place in Willy's mind. In this way, Miller fuses together two different kinds of set, and two different ways of using space.

THE UNNATURALNESS OF NATURALISM

Strictly speaking, the age of naturalism in the theatre was brief, from a little before 1880 to roughly 1900, but its knock-on effects and influence lasted much longer and continue to be felt today. The most famous playwrights associated with the movement are Ibsen, Strindberg and, less obviously, Chekhov. Ibsen's naturalistic phase lasted from *The Pillars of the Community* to *Hedda Gabler*, after which his writing became progressively more symbolist, although later plays such as *The Master Builder* and *Little Eyolf* have some naturalistic features. Strindberg's major naturalistic plays are *The Father* and *Miss Julie*, the latter being accompanied by an important Preface, in effect a manifesto of theatrical naturalism. Strindberg's break with naturalism, however, beginning with *The Dance of Death*, was more extreme than Ibsen's. His later plays are usually described as 'expressionist'. Chekhov's plays are less purely or strictly naturalistic than those of Ibsen and Strindberg, having 'poetic' (although they were written in prose) and symbolist aspects, however understated these are. Even so, plays such as *The Seagull*, *Three Sisters* and *The Cherry Orchard* are extraordinary as perfectly captured 'slices of life'. Moreover, Chekhov's plays were originally directed by Stanislavski who, more than anyone else at the time, was responsible for transforming the nature of acting, making it less histrionic and more natural.

Broadly speaking, naturalism in the theatre involves the *rejection of all kinds of theatricality*. Since its superficial goal is to represent a lifelike world or scene on stage, anything that draws attention to the artifice of the theatre is undesirable. For this reason, characters in naturalistic plays do not speak in heightened verse but in everyday prose, and they do not make asides or soliloquies. This is also the basic reason behind the full set, which 'covers over' the traces of the stage itself. In his Preface to *Miss Julie*, Strindberg argues that the set should be made as realistic as possible. Doors should not flap when slammed and kitchen shelves with pots and pans on them should be real, not painted.

The big question here is, Why? Did the naturalist playwrights imagine that an audience could be fooled into believing it was watching real people in a real room? This is most unlikely. To understand the real reason, we need to examine the way in which, in a naturalistic play, the audience is situated in relation to the action.

It is not surprising that most naturalistic plays are set in rooms rather than in streets or forests or mountainsides (although Chekhov sets parts of *The Seagull*, *Three Sisters* and *The Cherry Orchard* outside). Since the plays were written for theatres with a 'picture frame stage' (often also called the 'Italian stage,' because it first appeared in Italy in the early sixteenth century), the stage area is already a kind of room and much easier to decorate convincingly as a room than as some exterior location. Now, the 'room' of the stage has just three walls, one at the rear and two at the sides. Its *fourth wall*, then, exists in imagination between the actors on stage and the audience in the auditorium, but the position of this 'fourth wall' is strongly marked by the proscenium arch that frames the stage.

The 'fourth wall' is essential to naturalism in the theatre, but it is a mistake to equate this concept with the particular theatre architecture that serves it best. In fact, a fourth wall can be created in any kind of playing space, even if the setting is not a room. It is created whenever the actors perform *as if they are ignoring the presence of the audience.*

The 'as if' is essential in this formulation, for the actors do not in fact ignore the audience. Obviously it would be disastrous if they really were to do so! Nonetheless, Stanislavski tried to train his actors to achieve a state of what he called 'public solitude' when on stage. They should be able to act (the term is intentionally ambiguous here) as if they were entirely alone, even when watched by a myriad of eyes. One of the means of achieving public solitude involves what Stanislavski called 'circles of attention'. The actor learns to focus his attention on the details of what immediately surrounds him, or that which extends a little further, or that which includes the full stage area. Now, a full set helps greatly in such focusing. In general, in fact, we can say that a full set is more useful in helping the actors believe in the reality of the scene than it is in helping the audience to believe this. Furthermore, such belief on the part of the actors helps them establish the fourth wall more fully and effectively.

Playwrights such as Ibsen who wrote lengthy stage directions describing their intended sets probably did not do so for the reason just outlined, at least not consciously. Ibsen tends to use his sets as symbolic extensions of the themes of the play. For example, the large amount of furniture and the many bouquets of flowers that the audience sees at the start of *Hedda Gabler* establish a sense of a claustrophobic environment which reflects the way Hedda is 'trapped' in a loveless marriage. However, a convergence of interests seems to occur here. The kinds of naturalistic domestic dramas that Ibsen wrote certainly work best by excluding from them all sense of a watching audience and his sets function to this end.

It is important to realize that, in the context of the history of theatre, naturalism is an aberration. It is quite unnatural in the theatre to exclude all recognition of the presence of an audience from the play, although this recognition is often achieved much more subtly than by direct address by an actor. Moreover, it is a curious fact that, historically, naturalism in the theatre coincides more or less with the beginnings of the new medium of film or cinema. Cinema was soon to become a medium for drama, as was television later, *with a built-in fourth wall*. The actors in a movie can never truly acknowledge the *presence* of the audience since they are not in front of the audience. Only their recorded trace is in front of the audience, something literally dead (inanimate, at least) rather than *live*. In the light of this, we might go on to say that just as naturalism is a rejection or denial of theatricality, so it is a kind of denial of the *live-ness* of theatre. The invention of electrical stage lighting in the same period as naturalism contributed to the same end. Electrical stage lighting not only illuminates the stage, but it does so while plunging the auditorium into darkness. This helps the actors ignore the audience, it increases the 'psychological distance' between the audience and the action, and it even makes the audience relatively unconscious of itself. Lastly, the picture frame stage tends to reduce the three dimensions of the actual playing space to the appearance of two dimensions, quite unlike other arrangements such as the thrust or apron stage. This 'flattening' effect is enhanced by the way the picture frame stage slopes upward away from the audience (a feature which gives rise to the terms 'upstage' to indicate the rear of the stage and 'downstage' to indicate its front). In all these respects, the experience of watching a play in the theatre was turned into something more like the experience of watching a movie in a cinema, but before anyone had actual experience of the latter.

> ### 'THEATRICALITY BY THE BACK DOOR'
> Although naturalistic theatre rejects theatrical effects, it sometimes smuggles a kind of theatricality back into the play 'through the back door'. A good example is Ibsen's *A Doll's House*. In the later stages of this play, Nora's husband, Torvald, tells her to stop being 'theatrical' and behaving 'histrionically,' that is, to stop acting in an exaggerated way. To the audience, however, it is quite clear that Torvald is the one who overreacts to things and thus acts 'theatrically'. This is, of course, not true theatricality but the borrowed sense of the word which is applied in real-life situations. Even so, it is intended to have an ironic ring in a play. Something similar, though less clearly marked, occurs in *Hedda Gabler*. When, at the end of this play, Hedda shoots herself, Brack can only say that 'people don't do such things'. In other words, her behaviour has gone beyond the social norm. This hints at why Ibsen's naturalism rejects true theatricality: theatrical effects, which call attention to the artifice of performance, would detract from his intention to expose and deconstruct social *normality*.

BREAKING THE FOURTH WALL

It is not difficult to understand from its text alone if a play will establish or need or benefit from a fourth wall in performance. Some plays, however, establish a fourth wall initially and go on to break it later, a device which can have a powerful theatrical effect.

In Athol Fugard's *Statements After an Arrest Under the Immorality Act,* a white woman and 'coloured' man are involved in a sexual relationship which is illegal under one of the laws (the Immorality Act of the title) of Apartheid, the statutory system of separation of the races in South Africa between 1948 and 1993. In the first part of this play, the arrest has not yet taken place. Fugard focuses instead on the tensions within such a relationship, one in which different racial backgrounds imply widely divergent life experiences, expectations and opportunities, all creating their own difficulties, quite apart from the threat of possible arrest. Conflict inevitably arises. When this conflict reaches a temporary lull, far from a resolution, such that the man and woman can meet in an embrace, Fugard has a policeman enter to dictate a statement of the details of the arrest of the man and woman *to the audience*, thus breaking the fourth wall.

The effect here is complex. For the man and woman, the arrest has not yet happened, yet the policeman's statement refers to it in the past tense. The man and woman remain on-stage and in view, in a freeze. They are still in the back room of the small local library where the woman is librarian. The policeman, however, is presumed to be in the police station.

He dictates his statement to the audience as if the audience too has a role, that of police stenographer. This splitting of the onstage space is made possible by the fact that there is no set, only a blanket on which the man and woman lie. The back room of the library, moreover, is by now in almost complete darkness; its lights have been left off for secrecy and dusk has fallen. The policeman, thus, can appear in a strip of cold, bright light in the downstage area. He delivers his statement purely functionally, without emotion or any hint of character.

Why does Fugard do this? Although its title alerts the audience from the beginning to the play's true subject, the first part of the action allows the audience to forget or overlook the 'interest' the state takes in this particular love affair. The fourth wall, together with the basically naturalistic style of the action (even the minimal set is justified naturalistically, for the back room of the library has nothing in it), allows, even encourages, the audience to 'sit back' and start treating this as *any* love affair, however complicated by inequalities, perhaps to identify emotionally with either of the parties or simply to sympathize with both. Because of this, the policeman's entrance is much more of a shock. But more than this, what Fugard does is draw the audience's attention to its own role. The audience is not allowed to 'sit back' and vicariously to 'enjoy' this romance, however troubled. On the contrary, the audience is made *complicit*. Of course, this is not so crude a device as to imply that the audience itself is somehow responsible for the perverse laws of Apartheid. What it really implies is that since the state has taken upon itself the role of regulating the private business of erotic attraction and coupling, then a relationship like this one necessarily becomes a matter of public concern. That is, one cannot sit back and remain uninvolved.

Breaking the fourth wall like this has another effect in this play, for it makes possible a radical change of style in what follows. Immediately following the policeman's statement, the arrest takes place, but it is not represented naturalistically. No policeman is seen entering the back room of the library, only torch beams and camera flashes coming through a window. These torch beams and camera flashes are repeated three times, although they are *understood* to have happened only once; in between, the man and woman speak, or 'make statements,' but these are not the statements they are supposed to have made to the police – they are more like thoughts flashing through their heads, even though they sometimes interact with each other in what they say. Moreover, time is radically stretched in this part of the play, and a few moments of fictional time expand into many minutes of stage time. The important point here is this: such an 'expressionistic' style could not possibly have been introduced into an initially naturalistic play without the radical interruption, which breaks the fourth wall, and the 'flash forward' of the policeman's statement.

THE 'LAZZI OF DARKNESS'

Today, we take electrical stage lighting for granted. If a play text indicates that a scene takes place in darkness, as in Fugard's *Statements*, we expect lighting to be used to keep the stage as dark as possible while still preserving visibility. But 'staging darkness' was a very different matter before electrical stage lighting.

Lazzi are visual gags or comic routines which were used by the Commedia dell'Arte troupes that flourished in Europe between the sixteenth and eighteenth centuries. The famous '*lazzi* of darkness' were clowning routines in which the actors pretended that night had fallen and groped around the stage, bumped into each

> other, became terrified, discovered what they thought were dead bodies, put their hands accidentally down each other's trousers, and so on – all, of course, in the broad daylight in which the performance took place.
>
> A particularly gruesome scene (part of 4. 1.) in Webster's *The Duchess of Malfi* is set in darkness. Duke Ferdinand pretends that he wishes to be reconciled with his sister, the Duchess. However, since he has solemnly sworn never to look on her again, he asks that the lights of her room be removed. Then, in darkness, he offers her what he says is his hand, but what is in fact the severed hand of a corpse. Deceived, she kisses it. For a moment she thinks he must be ill, since his hand is so cold. Then horror dawns on her and she calls for lights. Since this play was originally performed indoors, some rudimentary lighting in the form of candles or torches and oil lamps would have been used, and some of this may well have been removed from the playing area by one of the Duchess's servants, then brought back. But the effect of this on actual visibility would have been negligible, such that the 'darkness' of the scene is imaginary.

BRECHTIAN THEATRE

Breaking the fourth wall is often associated with the work and ideas of the German marxist playwright, Bertolt Brecht. There is some truth in this, but it is quite commonly misrepresented. Brecht is often erroneously said to have wanted to 'remind' the audience that they were in a theatre, not watching real life. His actual work and ideas are much more subtle than this and much more important.

The techniques and goals of Brechtian theatre are worth knowing about because they have been adopted to greater or lesser degree by many dramatists who came after him. Brecht's central concept is usually called the 'alienation effect'. This is a rather unfortunate translation of the German *Verfremdungseffekt*, which is also sometimes rendered, more appropriately, as 'distanciation'. A more literal translation is the 'effect of making strange'. The idea behind it is that we are so accustomed to aspects of our society that we hardly even notice them, let alone think about how they might be changed. The role of the theatre, Brecht believed, is to represent aspects of our social life as though these are strange, so that the audience will see them as if for the first time and, as a result, begin to question them. Moreover, instead of becoming emotionally *involved* in the drama, the audience should be 'distanced' ('alienated') from it, so that it can adopt a critical attitude to the events and actions represented.

How can such an idea be mistaken for merely reminding the audience that it is in a theatre, and what, if anything, does it have to do with breaking the fourth wall? While an audience is never deluded or duped into believing that what it witnesses in the theatre is real life, however naturalistically this is represented, it can of course become very absorbed in the action by means of *identification* with one or some of the characters. When, for example, King Lear beats a servant, even servants in the audience may empathize with him and accept this, without really thinking about it, as 'what anyone would do in the circumstances'. Brecht believed that identification and empathy tended to override judgment. His so called 'alienation effects' are intended to prevent identification and empathy, at least to prevent them 'taking over'. Often, moreover, especially in Brecht's earlier work, these alienation effects do draw attention to the means of theatrical representation. But they do this in order to direct the audience's attention to the social reality that is being represented, something which is not in the theatre at all, but outside it. It is as though Brecht wants to say to his audience, 'What is being represented here is *real* rather than *realistic*; do not become so concerned with the representation, which is only a representation, that you forget that what *really* matters is what it is a representation of'. Moreover, breaking the fourth wall is often a part of this, since it draws the audience's attention to itself. For Brecht, the audience must be acknowledged as a participant in a collective project, one which involves using the theatre as a means to start thinking about changing the world.

Brecht is sometimes criticized, usually by critics who are hostile to his marxist politics, for not after all encouraging his audience to think about the world for themselves, which is what his theory claims, but telling them what to think about it instead. This is highly debatable, but if it is true at all, it is not true of his greatest plays. These tend to be 'criticized' in a more subtle way. Brecht's greatest plays, it is asserted, are great *in spite of his theory.* He was a 'true dramatist,' that is, creating complex, rounded characters and dramatically powerful plots, rather than a marxist pedagogue. *Mother Courage and her Children* in particular has received this kind of 'anti-Brechtian' acclaim.

Mother Courage was first performed at the Zurich Schauspielhaus, in neutral Switzerland, in 1941, during the darkest days of the Second World War, although the initial writing had been completed in 1939. Brecht reports that the play was hailed by the 'bourgeois press' as a tragedy demonstrating the 'vital strength of the mother animal'. As a result, he made a few changes to the original text to try to forestall such distortion (as he saw it), but some later critics have viewed the play in much the same way. It is worth trying to understand what lies behind this.

Brecht was opposed to the very idea of tragedy. In tragedy, human beings are presented as struggling against all-powerful fate. As a marxist, Brecht believed that human beings were not ultimately powerless, nor was anything in human life truly fated. Human beings may be products of the social world they live in, but the world they live in is itself the product of human beings – hence it can be changed. But actually changing it is far from simple.

Broadly speaking, the playwright's intention in *Mother Courage* is to direct the audience's attention to the nature of war. The Thirty Years War and the Second World War ultimately come down to the same thing, 'business by other means'. Mother Courage herself understands the commercial character of the war, says Brecht (in his notes to the play), as do most of the other characters. But she does not see beyond this. The masses, he asserts, learn as little from their experiences in such catastrophic situations as 'a scientist's rabbit learns of biology'. In other words, to Mother Courage and her like, things *do appear as fated*. But they should not appear as such to the audience. Brecht stresses that he has no obligation to make Mother Courage *see*, only to try to make the audience *see*. But see what? Basically, that the world does not have to be like this, that it could be otherwise.

It should be obvious that the very feature of the play which allowed the Swiss bourgeois press to acclaim it as a tragedy is the fact that Mother Courage herself 'does not see'. If, instead, Brecht had made his protagonist learn for herself and go on to articulate what he wanted the audience to see, the critics would not have been able to misunderstand his intentions in the way that they did. But by the same token, he would have *misrepresented* something in the social and historical reality which is his subject.

Brecht's 'experiment' in *Mother Courage* is a difficult one, but, contrary to those critics who think this play 'transcends Brechtianism,' it is at the heart of the project of his theatre. The basic question he is trying to answer is, how can the audience be led or invited or provoked to see things 'in the right way' without having any character do this on their behalf?

The actual 'alienation effects' in *Mother Courage* are of two kinds. Firstly, each scene except the last (there are twelve in all) is preceded by a synopsis of its content or principal interest. This might be projected as a caption or spoken by an actor. The device functions to prevent the audience feeling anything like suspense, since it is told what is coming, and to direct its attention to certain things. Being 'outside the action' (in the way that the words of a story-teller are outside the action of the story s/he tells), an evident artifice is created. Secondly, in some scenes the characters sing. This in itself is not an 'alienation effect,' since people sing in real life situations too, something that can easily be imitated in a play. Here, though, there is an intentional 'unnaturalness' about the way characters turn to song, although this is not as evident *in the text* of this play as it is in the texts of some of Brecht's earlier plays. We know from Brecht's theoretical writings that he preferred songs to function as interruptions to or breaks in the action rather than as continuations or extensions of the action, but he applied this idea more subtly as his work matured. Usually, the song is what matters, not any accompanying choreography and certainly not the 'psychology' behind the fact that a character has 'broken into song,' (Brecht ridiculed that moment in musicals where the character so obviously 'feels a song coming on'). More precisely, Brecht uses song as a device for focusing attention on its lyrics, and everything else takes on a temporary background role. The lyrics of the song both relate to and *extend* the significance of the scene in which they are sung, in a way that is analogous to the odes sung by the chorus in Greek tragedy (where the action is also temporarily 'suspended').

Caryl Churchill's *Vinegar Tom*, a play about a witch hunt set in seventeenth century rural England, is episodic in structure and comprises twenty-one short scenes. Between some of these scenes, a song is sung. Churchill stresses that the songs must not be sung by actors in character, nor even in costume. The songs are wholly modern in style, with lyrics that 'update' the subject matter of the play and draw attention to the continuing oppression of women. Fairly obviously such songs constitute alienation effects which interrupt the action (more than would a simple scene change) and provoke thought about the social reality being presented.

The question which arises here is whether an audience really needs such a device to help it grasp the analogy between the persecution of some women as witches three hundred years ago and the oppression of women today by other means and in other ways. No doubt this depends upon the audience itself. However, a further effect is achieved by these songs which goes beyond Brecht's ideas. But it is not easy to see this on the page. In being sung by actors out of character and out of costume, the songs become a 'gesture of solidarity' from the actors to the audience. They communicate that the actors are not simply performers impersonating fictional characters, but politically conscious and committed individuals whose purpose in presenting the play is to improve the world we live in. The songs thus provide a counterweight to the 'negative' side of the dramatized story. That is, the story is one of victimization and defeat, necessarily so, for to present anything like a 'heroic fight-back and victory' by the accused women would be a distortion of history. The songs prevent this generating a sense of pessimism or defeatism by transforming the theatrical event into a shared experience of solidarity and resistance. In a case like this, it is important to see that the play, as a performance or theatrical event, goes beyond the drama, that is, the story that it tells.

VISIBLE AND INVISIBLE ACTORS

In many plays, the actor is required to be *invisible*. What this means is that the attention of the audience should remain focused entirely on the character in the drama and not at all on the actor who is playing the character. If the audience's attention is drawn to the actor at work, say by a 'wooden' interpretation of the role or by a loss of concentration, some of the necessary 'illusion' is lost and pleasure in the drama is spoiled. But this is not true of all plays.

In Caryl Churchill's *Cloud Nine*, a number of devices draw attention to the actor as distinct from the character and this contributes greatly to the significance of the play. One of these devices is cross-casting or 'casting against character'. In Act One, which is set in nineteenth century Africa, Betty, the wife of the colonial administrator, Clive, is played by a man. The black servant, Joshua, is played by a white actor. Betty's and Clive's young son, Edward, is played by a woman. And Victoria, their baby daughter, is 'played' by a doll!

At times in the history of theatre when women were forbidden to be actors (as in ancient Athens or Elizabethan England), female parts were necessarily played by men or boys. The audience at such times would not have thought of this as having any significance in relation to the play but would simply have accepted it as a practical necessity, although Shakespeare sometimes plays with the convention by having a young female character, like Viola in *Twelfth Night*, dress up as a boy, and Aeschylus makes both the chorus and the Watchman in *Agamemnon* comment on how 'man-like' Clytemnestra is. Even so, what Churchill does here is closer to the more 'carnivalesque' tradition of the English Christmas pantomime, where, for example, the part of Prince Charming in *Cinderella* is played by a 'principal boy,' that is, a young woman, and the Ugly Sisters are played by 'pantomime dames,' that is, male comedians, such that the 'cross-dressing' involved is very visible. But it goes beyond even this, for the audience of *Cloud Nine* is required to grasp the logic behind the cross-casting. Betty is played by a man because, as a 'good wife,' she has internalized the male point of view. Similarly, Joshua is played by a white actor because he has been indoctrinated that white people are superior and is trying to deny his native roots. Edward is played by a woman because he has not yet managed to take on the gender role of 'young man' prescribed for him by his father. As for Victoria, she is simply an object.

Act Two is set in contemporary London some one hundred years later, yet it involves some of the same characters who have aged by only twenty-five years. For its second part, the play is also re-cast in a way that is intended to suggest how these characters have grown. In particular, Betty is now played by a woman, for she has left Clive and is in the process of coming to terms with her true self, and Edward, who is homosexual, is played by a man. Certain new characters are introduced, among them a five year-old girl who is played by a full-grown, preferably tall, strong and athletic man. The point of this is to bring out the energy and powerful presence of a child, something parents often try to suppress, especially when they want a 'pretty little girl' instead.

What Churchill does in this play is to develop and play with an idea which links theatre to life, an idea encapsulated in Shakespeare's famous "All the world's a stage". In life, we play roles. Hence we are like actors. Playing roles often involves trying to be what others want us to be. In this, the roles we play can be repressive. But once we see that we are playing roles, we can begin to experiment with different roles as a way of getting a little closer to 'who we really are'. The 'playfulness' involved in this is liberating. Then, when we discover who we really are, we discover that the roles we once felt obliged to play, roles in which our real selves were denied, are part of 'who we really are' too. Hence, at the end of the play, the Betty of Act Two meets and embraces the Betty of Act One, which symbolizes her full acceptance of herself.

Actors can be 'visible' in a play in a way that contributes to its significance for other reasons too. This occurs in what is called *poor theatre* or *rough theatre,* a theatre of minimal means which is necessarily *actor-centred.* Poor or rough theatre uses few, if any, props, little costume and no technical tricks. It is up to the actors to conjure up the setting and the action, including sound effects, using only their own bodies. If props are used, they tend to be multi-purpose and can signify quite different things depending on the way they are used. The more energetic and inventive the actors have to be to create the stage image, the more the audience will be aware of the actors at work, in a way that does not detract from the fiction but that may even add a layer of significance. This was discussed in the Introduction in relation to Athol Fugard's *The Island* and it applies equally to others among his 'Township Plays' such as *Sizwe Bansi is Dead*, where the energy and inventiveness of the actors comes to symbolize the suppressed potential of the black South African people under Apartheid.

It is worth noting that Shakespeare's theatre was a kind of 'poor theatre,' although costumes were often elaborate. Shakespeare too sometimes writes scenes which demand great physical inventiveness from the actors, such as the opening scene of *The Tempest*. The terrific storm that ends in shipwreck can hardly be conjured up by the mere rattling of thunder-sheets offstage, with actors shouting as though to be heard above the wind. With nothing, or very little, to represent the ship on stage, the *physical movement* of the actors becomes crucial. Performed well, a most impressive theatrical effect can be achieved. But is it *significant*, or does it remain a mere 'effect'? Arguably, in this case it is significant, for *The Tempest* is a special play that has the idea of illusion at its core and in which magic is a metaphor for theatre and theatre is a metaphor for magic. A brilliant but obviously theatrical illusion in Act 1, Scene 1 is a perfect start, laying a foundation for the audience's 'imaginative belief' that will help it accept a very strange world of spirits and spells through the rest of the play.

Lastly, Peter Shaffer's *Equus* is about a teenage boy, Alan, who is being treated by a psychiatrist, Dysart, because he has blinded six horses. In the film version of this play, real horses are shown, but in the theatre the horses are played by actors wearing abstract metal masks suggestive of horses' heads. In such a case, the actor is obviously 'visible'. Now, the point of this is not to solve – or avoid – the problem of having real horses onstage, since the blinding scenes could have been left as offstage action. Rather, it draws our attention to the *symbolic* value that horses have for Alan. While he blinds horses, Alan also worships them; Equus is his horse god, in fact. The use of human actors gives the horses in the story precisely the strange, ritual significance required.

CAN ANYTHING BE STAGED?

The Tempest begins with a shipwreck. Act Seven of Kalidasa's *The Recognition of Sakuntala* opens with King Dusyanta in a flying chariot coming out of heaven. As long as it is not required to be 'realistic,' it seems that theatre can stage any imaginable scene.

'Imaginable' is a key word here. The audience's imagination is a powerful resource of theatre, but it cannot work on its own. There must always be something 'natural' or 'life-like' at the core of the theatrical representation of the most weird and wonderful events and scenes. However, it is obvious that staging a shipwreck or an earthquake (as in Soyinka's *The Bacchae of Euripides: A Communion Rite*) or the Battle of Agincourt (in Shakespeare's *Henry V*) cannot be done naturalistically. The more it is necessary to engage the imaginative participation of the audience, the less naturalistic and the more openly theatrical the representation will be.

We saw earlier, in Chapter One, that many plays make use of offstage actions and events which either precede or happen during the main onstage dramatic action. We also saw that this can help to achieve dramatic compression and an intensification of the drama. Furthermore, the 'offstage reality' of a play is necessarily constructed by means of words. The principle that 'anything can be staged' represents the *opposite pole* to this. If indeed anything can be staged, then, in a sense, there is no practical need to leave certain events offstage. But although this is so, actually staging them might cause a breakdown of structure (especially if the play is climactic) or a breakdown of the prevailing conventions (especially where these tend towards naturalism). Note also that if a playwright chooses to write into the text a scene such as a shipwreck, its effectiveness in the theatre will be more physical than verbal, even if the playwright is Shakespeare! That is, the energy and skills of the actors will count for more than the dialogue in making it convincing. Moreover, although something like a shipwreck or earthquake is 'dramatic' in a certain sense, drama in the more important sense may well be rendered of secondary importance to the precise extent that the audience's attention is drawn to the theatricality of the representation. The essential difference here is this: a truly dramatic moment in the theatre is always the culmination of some kind of build up in the action, and it is like the tip of an iceberg; on the other hand an impressive theatrical effect, even if significant, is always immediate, created in the 'here and now' of the live theatrical event.

WRITING EXERCISE:
'IS THIS A DAGGER – OR NOT?'

There are three stages to this exercise, which is intended to raise questions about how theatrical writing engages the imaginative participation of the audience.

Firstly, write a monologue in which a character is speaking to someone by telephone, about whatever subject you like. Since this is a monologue, we do not hear any responses, although we may infer what these are from the words of the speaker.

Secondly, rewrite this monologue so that it is no longer spoken into a phone but to an unseen – and unheard – character who is now presumed to be in the same room as the speaker. Whereas the first monologue can be thought of as being purely dramatic, that is, as having no 'theatricality,' here the theatrical effect required is that the audience should be stimulated to imagine the presence of the other character. The key question to ask here is: does anything in the original monologue have to be changed, and if so why?

Thirdly, rewrite the second monologue so that it will be understood by the audience to be the speech of a madman who is deluded that someone else is present and replying to him! Note then that this is in effect to 'delete' the theatricality of the previous version and to make the scene once again purely dramatic, although very different from the original telephone conversation. Again, does anything in the second monologue need to be changed, and if so why?

This exercise is named after Macbeth's soliloquy, "Is this a dagger which I see before me," where the audience fully understands that Macbeth is deluded. The point is

> that in the theatre such dramatic delusions can be transformed into theatrical 'realities'. The difference may lie only in the context, that is, in the audience's understanding of the governing conventions of the performance, or it may lie in the way the scene has actually been written.

THE FUNCTION OF THE STORY-TELLER

In Chapter One, we saw that offstage events can come to affect the main onstage action by being reported to onstage characters. Where this happens, the character who reports such events becomes a *messenger*, if only temporarily. The 'function of the messenger' is defined by the fact that the report is made *to other characters* within the drama, such that the audience gains important information only indirectly. The 'function of the story-teller,' on the other hand, is defined by the fact that a character or an actor tells some part of the story *directly to the audience.*

The function of the messenger is dramatic, for the report is itself an event within the action of the play. The function of the story-teller is theatrical, for the telling of some part of the story directly to the audience is not an event within the action. A story-teller is either continuously outside the action or moves in and out of it, becoming a character within the story as enacted on stage as well as, at other times, a story-teller outside it. A single story-teller may be used to frame the whole action, as in Brecht's *The Caucasian Chalk Circle,* or the role may be 'distributed' so that any of the actors can step out of character as necessary in order to provide the audience with background information, as in David Hare's *Stuff Happens*.

In plays, the function of the story-teller is not only a convenient device for providing essential information and for promoting the continuity of the action (for a very brief intervention by a story-teller can allow one scene to 'dissolve' easily into another), but it also tends to 'distance' the action, undermining the 'illusion' and drawing attention to the artifice of performance. This is especially important in a play like *Stuff Happens* which enacts not a fiction, but a 'documentary drama' of the run up to the American and British invasion of Iraq in March 2003. Here, story-telling by actors (out of character) not only produces the 'artificial' context in which actors can impersonate characters such as George W. Bush, Donald Rumsfeld and Tony Blair, without needing to be perfect likenesses, but also facilitates the smooth transitions necessary for a drama covering many countries and involving no less than forty-four named characters!

However, a play which uses a story-teller will fail as a play if the *enacted* action never seems to 'come to life' onstage independently of the story-telling. The action, that is, is never a mere illustration of the story being told, but remains its essence, as in all forms of true theatre. This is not true of the actual art of oral story-telling, which seems to have existed in all societies and cultures, and which also involves some elements of performance. In oral story-telling, the story-teller 'enacts' different roles and actions in a limited way, for example by mimicking a tone of voice or gesture. But where actors other than the story-teller are used the situation is very different. Those actors are *equally real* as theatrical means, and the story as they enact it is always something more than the story as it is narrated.

> **WRITING EXERCISE:**
> **THE STORY STRIKES BACK!**
>
> This is a difficult exercise which, if done well, produces very interesting scenes. It focuses on the relationship between that which is narrated and that which is enacted in a scene, and on the relationship between the story-teller and the characters in the story.
>
> Imagine a story-teller who can 'call up' actors like 'living props' to enact parts of the story that s/he tells. Start writing this scene, beginning with some pure story-telling. But as it goes on, something strange begins to happen. The acted characters begin to take over by acting 'outside the story' as it is told, not exactly as the story-teller says they do, or should. What does the story-teller do? At first, s/he may change the story to fit what is actually happening, but at a certain point s/he will have to intervene, entering into the story himself or herself to bring it back on track. How do the characters react to this?
>
> In this exercise, oral story-telling is turned into true theatre, for a basic principle of theatre is that it has no single controlling voice.

The policeman in Fugard's *Statements After an Arrest Under the Immorality Act* is a kind of story-teller, but not like those discussed above. He is a story-teller who behaves like a messenger, for although he narrates an account of the arrest directly to the audience, he does so in a way that 'casts' the audience as a kind of character in the drama. His narration is dramatically motivated as a dictation to a police typist, whereas the narrations of most story-tellers are not motivated in this way.

THE 'THEATRICAL METAPHOR'

By the 'theatrical metaphor' I mean any way in which a playwright makes significant use of the analogy between theatre and life, either explicitly or implicitly. We have already seen it at work in Churchill's *Cloud Nine* where the way the action is presented by 'visible actors' reflects the significance of role play in human life. But it arises in many other ways or forms. The following paragraphs will suggest a few of these.

In Aeschylus' *Agamemnon*, all Clytemnestra's onstage actions are 'framed' by the presence of the chorus of old men, which is a kind of hostile audience for her. To dominate this chorus, she has to act – that is, to *perform* – in a powerful way. Moreover, she opts to humiliate her husband by making a public speech of welcome, itself a 'theatrical' act. She then 'stages' a scene by having a rich tapestry laid for him to tread upon (tempting him in this way to commit hubris). In short, her great *theatrical* presence in the play is not just a consequence of her passionate nature but grows out of her *dramatic* situation, a woman in a man's world, which, given her desire for revenge, effectively requires her to act like this.

In Euripides' *The Bacchae*, the god Dionysos tempts King Pentheus to dress as a woman in order to go and spy on the Bacchants. Here, there is an obvious analogy with the taking on of roles and the use of costume to this end in theatre. In his version of the play, Soyinka puts this 'robing' scene onstage, where Euripides leaves it offstage. But we do not see in this just the way in which 'theatre' arises in the donning of costume. We also see in Pentheus a man whose rigid masculinity is self-repressive and who has a deep desire to go beyond his own too narrow definition of himself.[1]

Many characters in plays 'act' in order to appear something they are not, or believe they are not, revealing in this way something that they are. Hamlet pretends to be mad – so successfully at times that he may really be mad, if only temporarily. Shakespeare sometimes has his heroines dress up as boys, young men or eunuchs, like Viola in *Twelfth Night*. The very fact that they can get away with this and even have other female characters fall in love with them raises questions about what gender – as distinct from sex[2] – really is.

Ben Jonson's Volpone is a confidence trickster. He pretends to be seriously ill so that others rush to bring him valuable gifts in the hope of being made his heir. The pleasure he takes in this lies not so much in material gain as in the skill with which he pulls off the trick, that is, it lies in the performance itself. At one point he pretends to be a mountebank, a street peddler of quack medicines, in order to catch a glimpse of Corvino's wife, Celia. This requires considerable performance skill on his part, for mountebanks were as much street entertainers as they were sellers. His delight in 'theatrical' changeability is expressed in extreme form when, later, he tries to seduce Celia by picturing their love-making to come:

> Then will I have thee in more modern forms,
> Attired like some sprightly dame of France,
> Brave Tuscan lady, or proud Spanish beauty;
> Sometimes, unto the Persian Sophy's wife,
> Or the Grand Signor's mistress; and, for change,
> To one of our most artful courtesans,
> Or some quick Negro, or cold Russian;
> And I will meet thee in as many shapes:
> Where we may so transfuse our wandering souls
> Out at our lips, and score up sums of pleasures. (3. 7. 226-235)

But this is hardly likely to appeal to Celia, even were she not the virtuous, chaste wife that she is! Volpone says nothing here to praise her beauty or her person, but merely invites her to share in his fantasies, fantasies that amount to little more than a need for sexual variety. What Jonson is clearly suggesting here is that the 'theatricality' of Volpone is a kind of perversity or at least of unnaturalness.

A 'play within a play,' as occurs in *Hamlet* or *A Midsummer Night's Dream*, serves to draw our attention in a straightforward way to the relation or 'continuity' between theatre and life. In *The Winter's Tale*, Shakespeare extends the underlying idea of this device in an extraordinarily theatrical yet at the same time subtle way. When, at the end of this play, the statue of Hermione 'comes to life,' a 'magical' theatrical effect is achieved. To interpret it as something more than this, that is, to make sense of it within the dramatic action

---

[1] In Euripides' play, Pentheus consents to be dressed as a woman and even desires it. In Soyinka's, he does not; he believes he is being dressed in his armour, while in fact he is being dressed as a woman. For this reason the 'theatrical metaphor' is stronger in Euripides' play.

[2] This term is commonly misused. A person is male or female; this is not their gender, but their sex. A person's gender is a role, their masculinity or femininity. Sex is biologically given, but gender is socially and culturally constructed. But this does not mean that it is always easy to distinguish between sex and gender in practice.

of the play, we need to infer that Paulina has kept Hermione alive for the last sixteen years, when everyone else, including the audience, thought that she was dead. In effect, Paulina has manipulated the action in the way that a playwright or theatre director can do, and it is she that 'stages' the final scene. She does this principally for the 'audience' of Hermione's husband, Leontes. His amazement and that of the actual audience coincide. He is transformed in and through the experience, absolved of all guilt for his earlier jealousy – but so too, if to a lesser extent, is the audience in the theatre, which experiences its own complete redemption or release from the earlier, very dark world of this play. While we realize that what we have been watching is 'just a play,' we also see that it has had contained within it a kind of 'play within a play,' not literally and not one that simply reflects or mirrors life, but one that actually *changes* life.

QUESTIONS TO ASK ABOUT YOUR SET PLAYS

1. Does the significance of the play lie entirely in the represented action and dialogue, or has the playwright used any of the other means of theatre in a way that contributes to this significance?
2. How is the real performance space used to represent fictional locations?
3. Does the play seem to have been written for a particular kind of theatre?
4. What kind of set is required by the play?
5. What props does it need? Can anything in the action be mimed?
6. Does the play seem to need a fourth wall in performance? If so, does it go on to break the fourth wall at any point?
7. Does the play contain any 'alienation effects,' that is, devices intended to prevent the audience getting too involved in the action or identifying too much with the characters? If so, why?
8. Are songs used? If so, how do they relate to the action and what is their purpose?
9. Should the actors be 'invisible' throughout? If not, what is the significance of the way we are invited to see the actor as well as the character?
10. How 'realistically' should events within the play be staged? If the choice arises, are there events that might be better staged non-realistically?
11. Does the play contain events that cannot be staged realistically? If so, does the text make clear just how they are to be staged or not?
12. To what extent and in what ways does the play make use of the imagination of the audience?
13. Are there any story-tellers? If so, is this role consistently given to one actor/character or distributed among many? Does the story-teller tell the story as an actor or as a character? Is the story-teller also a character in the story?
14. Does the play make use of the idea of theatre (or of plays, or of acting, or of performance), either explicitly or implicitly?

CHAPTER FIVE
DRAMA AND THEORY OF KNOWLEDGE

In their Theory of Knowledge course, IB Diploma students learn to question and generally to think about the nature and justification of knowledge claims. As a general rule, it is easier to understand both what knowledge is and how it is arrived at in the areas of mathematics and the sciences than it is in the area of the arts. Drama, of course, is an art. In this chapter, we will examine both the nature of drama as an area of knowledge, and if and how drama functions as a way of knowing.

DRAMA AS AN AREA OF KNOWLEDGE

It is easy to see that there is such a thing as *knowledge of drama*, just as there is knowledge of any art. The entire aim of this book is to communicate knowledge of drama. Knowledge of drama and of other kinds of literature is exactly what you, as a Language A1 student, have to acquire. In part this knowledge is fact-based, for as a bare minimum you need to know what happens in your set plays, but the more important part of it is skills-based, for the goal is critical analysis rather than mere description. In relation to some specific feature of a play rather than the play as a whole, the question which needs answering is not so much *what* did the playwright write, but *why* did s/he write it like this? Moreover, the ability to analyze plays texts critically tends to increase with experience, that is, with wider acquaintance with different kinds of play. As your experience increases, you become more aware of the different kinds of choices that writers have had. Thus, faced with a specific text, you become increasingly able to 'put yourself in the writer's shoes'. Then, insofar as you can justifiably claim to know what the writer is trying to achieve in any part of the play and why s/he does one thing rather than another, you have *understanding* – not the limited kind of understanding required merely to follow the plot and make sense of the action, but understanding of the nature of the art of drama.

Difficulties arise as soon as we ask what makes one play good, or better than another play, that is, when we try to *evaluate* the objects of study. Theory of Knowledge students often try to evade this question. They unthinkingly adopt a simplistic relativism, claiming that, in relation to artistic objects, judgments like *good* and *bad* are 'subjective' or just a 'matter of opinion'. This is reminiscent of the defensive assertion, "I know what I like". The subtext of this remark, of course, is 'And I don't have to justify my likes to you' – no doubt because the speaker doesn't know how to.

Justification is a key word here. If, initially, we distinguish our *values* from our *tastes*, we can say that our tastes are those of our 'likes' (such as a liking for chocolate) that we do not feel any need to justify, while our values are those of our 'likes' (such as a liking for the music of Beethoven or the paintings of Goya) that we might feel a need to justify in some circumstances. In this context, justification lies somewhere between *explanation* and *persuasion*. We do not necessarily want others to share our values (though sometimes we do), but we will tend to feel that an authentic justification of a value of ours ought in principle to have some persuasive power. If I like chocolate it is of no concern to me whether or not a friend of mine likes chocolate (except insofar as if she does not, then I don't have to share mine!), and for this very reason I would have no idea of *how* to persuade someone that chocolate is 'good'. But if I like Ben Jonson's *Volpone* and my friend does not, I may feel that there is a 'communication gap' between us in relation to something that matters, and in consequence of this I will feel that I really ought to be able to 'bridge that gap' by explaining why I think that *Volpone* is 'good' and possibly persuading her to share this view.

Suppose then that I try to do so. Her response is, "Now I see why *you* like *Volpone*, but I still don't". This means that although I have failed to persuade her to *like Volpone*, nonetheless I have *succeeded in justifying the value* I put on this play. Moreover, this is enough to bridge the communication gap that existed before.

It is crucial to understand that "Now I see why *you* like *Volpone*, but I still don't," is not in any way an assertion of relativism. It does not imply, 'What you like is good to you and what I like is good to me'. Instead it implies that there is a difference between *appreciation* and *liking*. Appreciation, we might say, is understanding not just that others like something but also why. In effect, I have persuaded my friend that Jonson's play is 'good,' which is implied by her now appreciating it, but I have not persuaded her to like it. I have communicated and justified the value I put on the play, but not the element of taste that continues to determine in part our likes and dislikes in the field of arts.

The distinction between appreciation and liking is essential if we are to get beyond relativism. It allows us to say that what we like is a 'subjective' matter while what we appreciate is not. (The relation between appreciation and liking is actually much more complex than this, since our tastes are often affected by what we learn to appreciate. In other words, our taste itself can become more 'educated'. For present purposes, however, we will rest content with the simplification.) What we appreciate is not a subjective matter because our faculty of appreciation is open to the justifications of values that can be made by others.

In relation to the arts as an area of knowledge, what matters is what we *appreciate* as good art, not what we like. Still, none of this tells us *how* justifications of artistic values can be made. To go further, we need another distinction. Any work of art embodies some kind of *intention* and is at the same time a more or less successful *realization* of that intention. Hence a work of art is evaluated on two levels, or in relation to two questions. Firstly, is its intention worthwhile? Secondly, has its intention been effectively realized?

It is important that we do not reduce the idea of a work of art's intention to the intention of the artist or writer, especially not to his or her conscious intention. Basically, this is because we are primarily – perhaps only – interested in how the intention is embodied or realized in the work itself.

The intention embodied in a work of art is something we can 'read off' from the work of art itself, although in some cases we may need other kinds of knowledge to help us do so, such as knowledge of other cultures or historical periods. Broadly, if its intention cannot be read off from the work itself, then that work has obviously failed to realize its intention. To the extent that we can read the intention off from the work, it is not a total failure; however, it may well be that the work could have realized its intention more effectively or more fully.

To give this a more concrete sense, let's imagine a discussion between an experienced theatre director and a new playwright. The theatre company for which the director works has decided to stage the playwright's first play, but only after it is rewritten to improve some of its faults….

DIRECTOR: First, the good news. We really think this play has possibilities, or I wouldn't be talking to you now. The basic idea is great. I mean, two surfers who only ever meet while riding the waves, well, the theatrical possibilities of staging that appeal to me. I think we can get a real WOW effect. Its very 'physical theatre'. That markets well among the young, apart from the obvious theme-appeal. But we don't want effect for effect's sake. Are you with me?

PLAYWRIGHT: Are we getting to the bad news?

DIRECTOR: The less good news.

PLAYWRIGHT: I didn't write the play just to 'wow' the audience. I wanted to 'stage the ocean' for symbolic reasons. I mean, that terrific power and that, I can't think of the word, that… profoundly unfathomable amorphousness that just 'takes shape' underneath us! We live in an age without gods, we need something bigger than us, something that can break us like a twig but which also holds us up, even upright, you know, but only as long as we live in the moment…. Maybe you've never surfed?

DIRECTOR: Actually, I think you've overdone the 'symbolic reasons'.

PLAYWRIGHT: But they're the point.

DIRECTOR: I know, and I approve the point. What I mean is, audiences don't like to be spoonfed. Think of Beckett. Full of symbolism. But does he tell the audience 'this is a symbol'?

PLAYWRIGHT: Do I?

DIRECTOR: Indirectly, yes. Look, this is easy enough to change. It isn't the main problem.

PLAYWRIGHT: I see. What is?

DIRECTOR: Your middle sags.

PLAYWRIGHT: Too much beer.

DIRECTOR: The middle's always the hard bit. You know, at the start of a play the audience is always on your side. If you lose them, it's ten times harder to get them back.

PLAYWRIGHT: I was thinking of building in a 'lift,' some kind of mini-climax, just before the interval. Then I thought, that's so passé. I could do it.

DIRECTOR: Hm. I don't think so.

PLAYWRIGHT: What else?

DIRECTOR: Well, this is the bad news. But you've got to look at it the right way. It'll make your play a lot more effective. Most of the middle, you see, is padding. Disposable. Cut it.

PLAYWRIGHT: But….

DIRECTOR: Exactly. With some of the other over-writing pruned back, it'll play at around forty-five minutes. What you've got here, you see, is a very good one-act play that's been spun out to full length. You idea's just not big enough, I'm afraid. That's not to say it's not a good idea… but we've been over that.

PLAYWRIGHT: A *one-act* play?

DIRECTOR: You're quite right. That is on the old-fashioned side, isn't it? But we'll make you a double-bill with a short Beckett or Pinter. Your name, I'm afraid, doesn't translate as bums on seats…. Still, it's a foot on the ladder.

PLAYWRIGHT: Look, I don't want to seem ungrateful or anything, but, frankly, I suspect *that's* the real reason you want me to cut so much, so it's not just my name on the play bills.

DIRECTOR: It's as I said, your idea's just not big enough. Every idea has its right treatment, its right staging, its right number of actors, its right duration. I'm telling you that you've got a good idea and you've nearly made it work. You're a new writer. That's why you think I'm telling you you've failed. I'm not. I'm telling you you've nearly succeeded. Nearly.

Now, the director's assertion that every idea has its right treatment is a variation on an old theme in the theory of art, that works of art are defined by a very close relation between *content* and *form*. This is sometimes referred to as the organic form of a work of art. It is sometimes claimed, in fact, that any change in the form of a true (i.e. fully successful) work of art results in a change of content. If this is true, it entails that we cannot actually discuss the content of a work of art, since to try to do so is to try to 'realize' that content outside its necessary form. For this reason, critics and theorists sometimes refer to the 'paraphrasable content' of a work of art, that is, a kind of reduced or simplified version of content that can be extracted. Note, then, that the director's point of view is a little different. By implication, he can know what the playwright's 'idea' is and hence can give advice about how best to realize that idea in the right form of play. Here, the term 'idea' refers to rather more than 'paraphrasable content,' since this idea *implies* a right form. It is much closer, in fact, to what I earlier called the 'intention' of the work of art.

(As a student of literature you are confronted by 'given' – published – works which may appear as 'unchangeable'. However, it is a good idea to put yourself imaginatively in the position of an editor or a director, to whom a text may appear as 'work in progress' requiring revision. You may even find some scenes in Shakespeare which can be improved so as to realize the play's or scene's idea more effectively!)

Students sometimes write or speak about the 'message' or the 'deeper meaning' of a play or other literary text. Usually, neither of these terms is appropriate and they should not be used as synonyms for a play's 'idea' or 'intention'. A message is something that can be communicated in different ways, via different channels or different media, without significant change to its nature as a message. Thus the concept implicitly denies the close relation between content and form in art. As for a work's deeper meaning, the problem lies in the metaphor of 'depth'. If this meaning is not grasped on a first reading, it is usually because the first reading is not very skillful or even very attentive and not because the author has somehow managed to 'bury' this meaning under the surface in some way. This concept misrepresents the nature of the complexity of works of art.

As said above, a work of art such as a play is evaluated on two levels, the level of its 'idea' or 'intention' and the level of its realization of this idea or intention. Up to a point, these levels can be correlated with the two major aspects of artistic value, *originality* and *skill*. The 'idea' itself is valued insofar as it is original, while its realization is valued insofar as this requires a certain skill. Still, this is something of an over-simplification, as we shall see.

It is considerably more difficult to recognize originality than it is to recognize skill. This is because, in the context of art, originality implies more than innovation. Innovation is simply newness and difference. Originality is *worthwhile* newness and difference. This begs a question: what exactly is worthwhile? In part, the answer is as follows: a work which is truly original in a given art form tends to involve a *strikingly appropriate but nonetheless unexpected way of using that particular art form*. In other words, artistic ideas are not 'original' in themselves, but only in relation to the nature of the art form or medium in which they are expressed. An original work of art is not simply one that expresses something new about the world we live in or about human life, but one which, *in order to do so*, seems to extend the expressive capacity of the art in which it is expressed. What is 'worthwhile' in this is on the one hand some kind of insight into the 'human condition' or contemporary society, and on the other hand the extension of the expressive capacity of the specific art form needed to convey that insight. Moreover, the latter seems to validate the former. That is, the insight seems to be 'true,' or at least worthwhile, *because* an extension of the expressive capacity of the specific art form was needed to express it.

Note, however, that this is a *modern* view of art. It is not how art was generally thought of before the Romantic period (which began towards the end of the eighteenth century). Very broadly speaking, the last two hundred years have seen increasing emphasis on originality and decreasing emphasis on skill, with 'art' becoming more strongly distinguished from 'craft'.

There is a very important problem associated with the concept that a work of art realizes or embodies an intention or idea. Consider, for example, Sophocles' *Oedipus the King*. This play was written and first performed over two thousand four hundred years ago in a culture with very different assumptions and beliefs than our own. When we read or see this play, we surely do not see it in the same way that its original audience did. How can we think of it as *embodying* an 'intention' when this may be perceived differently in different periods?

As was briefly mentioned above, sometimes we may need knowledge of other cultures in order to understand the original idea or intention of a play. Of course, it is debatable whether we can ever fully reconstruct how a play would have been understood by its original audience, since we necessarily see this too from our own culturally conditioned viewpoint. But more importantly, this kind of approach is not strictly necessary and may even be counter-productive. This is because *theatre is an art of the present*, not the past. While the classicist or historian may wish to understand the meaning *Oedipus* had in ancient Greece, the modern theatre director will see it as a play worth staging now, a play, that is, with *modern relevance*. These views of the same play are likely to be different. Nonetheless, there may still be some relation between them.

What makes an old play relevant today? The traditional view is that great art conveys unchanging or 'eternal' truths about human existence or human nature. Very few cultural theorists would subscribe to what they consider this 'naïve' view today. Instead they would argue that art is open to interpretation in a way that allows different ages to find different things in it. But can it be so simple?

Suppose, as a kind of thought experiment, that Sophocles had never written *Oedipus the King* but that a modern dramatist had written a play with the same plot and same story, even in much the same style. Would an audience watching the latter play have the same experience as when watching Sophocles' play? The answer is surely 'No,' for when we watch Sophocles' play today, part of the experience – and, by the same token, part of the meaning of the play for us – lies in our awareness that it is an old play that comes to us from a different culture, and we both interpret it and react to it in this context. Of course, this is not to say that we can access its original meaning. Rather, its cultural 'strangeness' or 'otherness' is part of its meaning for us. But this strangeness cannot be absolute, for if it were we would not feel that there was any common ground between the play's apparent concerns and our own. Such common ground must exist for the play to seem relevant. At the same time, it is a common ground conceived or treated differently in the play, in a way that does not simply *mirror* our own culturally conditioned interests, but *extends* them.

Sometimes it is easy to specify the common ground between our own concerns and those of an old play. Medea's sense of betrayal by Jason or Othello's jealousy or Nora's desire for individual autonomy are immediately recognizable by twenty-first century audiences. Sometimes, however, the common ground is not so straightforward. This is the case with *Oedipus*, in spite of Freud's appropriation of the story which has made it a modern myth. It is alien to modern assumptions that Oedipus should accept full responsibility, to the extent of blinding himself, for killing his father and marrying his mother, not so much because these things were preordained as because they were committed in ignorance. Oedipus would hardly be held responsible in a modern court of law, except perhaps for his 'road rage' in killing a 'road hog' (who happened to be his father). But this is really the point. This play *challenges* our understanding of the relationship between action, intention and responsibility, and much of its relevance lies in this.

The problem of relevance has another dimension. While *Oedipus the King* is obviously much more distant culturally than *A Doll's House*, nonetheless among the myths of western culture is the idea that western culture itself began in ancient Greece. While modern education puts far less emphasis on this than was the case a hundred years ago, we are still led to believe that ancient Greek tragedies belong to 'our' tradition, that is, if we identify with western culture ourselves. The other side of this coin is that a western theatre company tends to be much more reluctant to stage a Japanese Noh play, seeing this as too alien to attempt, than it is an ancient Greek play. If it is attempted, as is sometimes the case, it is usually with a greater consciousness of adapting the Noh play to a western audience.

In fact, the complex nature of the relevance of old plays is often reflected in the practice of adaptation. Adaptation is much more common in the theatre than it is in other arts. Only very rarely do modern painters rework the paintings of old masters and, as far as I know, no novelist has bothered to rewrite *War and Peace*, but many playwrights have adapted old plays. Eugene O'Neill's *Mourning Becomes Electra* (a reworking of Aeschylus' *The Oresteia*), Jean Anouilh's *Antigone*, Wole Soyinka's *The Bacchae of Euripides: A Communion Rite* and Yukio Mishima's *Five Modern Noh Plays* are just a few examples. Such adaptation implies two things: firstly, the original play is relevant today; secondly, it is not relevant enough. Put differently, the relevance of the original play can only be brought out fully by adapting it.

Where a play is an adaptation, it is useful to compare it with the original and to try to understand the specific intention behind the adaptation. This intention is variable, as is the nature or degree of adaptation itself. *Mourning Becomes Electra* updates (but not to full contemporaneity) Aeschylus' powerful story of a family curse, setting it during the American civil war. This entails reworking the mythic and supernatural dimensions of the original and replacing them with a modern sense of abnormal psychology. O'Neill's intention in this is not to recreate the ancient idea of fate but to find a modern analogue for it.

Anouilh does not update Sophocles' story but gives it a different emphasis. Basically, his Creon his less combative than in the original and his Antigone is more so. Thus we no longer have an 'unwinnable' conflict between individuals each with unshakeable beliefs but between a dispassionate commitment to civic responsibility and the desire to subvert or go beyond it. Through this Anouilh both reasserts the idea of tragedy, as a timeless truth of human existence, and indirectly 'celebrates' resistance to authority (especially, of course, the actual resistance to the Nazi occupation of France).

As its title implies, *The Bacchae of Euripides: A Communion Rite* 'contains' Euripides play. But it also builds on the original, adding and extending scenes and relating the play to the existence of slavery. Through this, Soyinka aims both to bring out the full religious power and intensity of the original and to extend its significance politically. To the latter end, he builds greatly on the sense in which Dionysos is the god of the marginalized and the displaced.

The Five Modern Noh Plays of Mishima are an attempt to 'reinvent' a traditional genre for a rapidly and radically changing society. Each of the five is based on a traditional Noh play, but the reworking of the story and setting is extensive. Moreover, the performance style of Noh – which is a highly stylized form of dance drama – is dropped, as are the traditional role types. Most importantly, the often overt Buddhist (or sometimes Shinto) content of Noh is discarded. All this has to be seen in the context of the trauma of Japan's defeat in 1945 and its reconstruction under strong American influence. Mishima, who was strongly committed to many traditional Japanese values, is trying in these plays to preserve the mystery and poetic suggestiveness of the medieval originals but in a modern form without any archaic or nostalgic artificiality.

Perhaps the reason that adaptation is common in theatre is that, as a live performance art, theatre is necessarily an art of the present. Every production or staging of a play, old or new, is an 'adaptation' of sorts, emphasizing some things and downplaying others, aimed at bringing out its modern relevance.

DRAMA AS A WAY OF KNOWING

Traditionally, the arts have been seen as means of formulating and communicating certain kinds of knowledge. The knowledge in question here is not knowledge of art itself, but knowledge of other things, such as human nature or virtue, which may be obtained through the experience of art. But note that if it is true that works of art embody and communicate knowledge of things other than art, then knowing how they do so becomes a necessary part of the knowledge of art.

As far as (serious) drama is concerned, Aristotle argues in the *Poetics* that its purpose is to show us 'universals'. He explains this by contrasting the jobs of dramatist and historian. The historian describes particulars; for example, what a specific individual did or said. The dramatist, on the other hand, shows us what a certain kind of individual will probably or necessarily do or say in certain circumstances. Moreover, Aristotle asserts that the knowledge thus provided by the dramatist is more 'philosophical,' hence more important than the knowledge provided by the historian, for it is knowledge of the general principles of human nature.

This view of drama has held currency in many later periods, even if it does not do so in our own. It is excellently expressed by Dr Johnson, in his *Preface to Shakespeare* (1765):

> Nothing can please many, and please long, but just representations of general nature. Particular manners can be known to few, and therefore few only can judge how nearly they are copied. The irregular combinations of fanciful invention may delight awhile by that novelty of which the common satiety of life sends us all in quest; but the pleasures of sudden wonder are soon exhausted, and the mind can only repose upon the stability of truth.

As for Shakespeare himself, his characters…

> are not modified by the customs of particular places…. His persons act and speak by the influence of those general passions and principles by which all minds are agitated…. In the writings of other poets, a character is too often an individual: in those of Shakespeare it is commonly a species.

Now, many modern readers will wonder at the last sentence quoted. Doesn't Shakespeare's greatness lie, at least in part, in the way he creates complex, 'three-dimensional' characters who seem true *individuals* rather than *types*? This is the view of Shakespeare that became established during the Romantic period, some forty or fifty years after Johnson wrote, and it has held sway ever since.

To make sense of this, we first need to accept that what we see in a work of art is partly determined by our own assumptions and predilections. But although this is so, there is probably less difference between Johnson's perspective and the later view than superficially appears to be the case. What we mean by a 'type,' which is a simplification of character, is not the same as what Johnson means by a 'species,' which is not. Similarly, Johnson's use of the term 'individual' does not imply the kind of complexly individuated sense of character that we value so highly, but rather a character who seems too tied to and defined by a particular time and place. Still, this does not mean that 'under the surface of the words used' we are really valuing the same thing in Shakespeare as Johnson did, for this is not true. It is false not so much because we have a different idea of what 'human nature' is, but because we have a different idea of *what kind of concept* 'human nature' is.

Today, intellectuals tend to shy away from the concept of 'human nature' (unless they are 'social biologists' or geneticists). In the prevailing modern view, 'human nature' is not fixed and changeless, as Johnson thought is was, but a variable which is very largely conditioned by social and cultural circumstances. We have recognized, moreover, that specific claims about what human nature is always imply a political programme, for they imply that a certain kind of social structure conforms best with human nature. In the 'orthodox' modern view, this is enough to make such claims suspect.

In the modern view, moreover, works of art do not provide access to some general truth that lies beyond any individual point of view, as Johnson believed they did or could. On the contrary, we often value art for the very way it inscribes such individual points of view. Pinter's plays, for example, are highly rated not because they reveal 'what human beings are really like,' but because they consistently, even ruthlessly develop and elaborate a valid 'way of looking' at human behaviour. Someone may find this 'Pinteresque' view more congenial than that of Peter Shaffer, which implies that *for such a person* Pinter expresses more 'truth'. However, such a person will not think of Pinter as expressing *the truth*. As for *the truth*, this tends to be thought of as many sided, such that no individual dramatist, not even Shakespeare, can express it. For a given person then, 'the truth' may be distributed among – or between – Harold Pinter, David Mamet, Brian Friel and so on, but *not* Tom Stoppard and Alan Ayckbourn.

Even so, the underlying assumption of the modern view is still that works of art like plays *tell us something*. They are not just entertainment. What they tell us does not consist of specific facts or 'information' (which Aristotle and Johnson did not believe either), but nor does it consist of 'universals' or general rules. Rather, plays provide us with 'interpretative models' of human life, which we judge not so much in terms of their accuracy or verisimilitude (which implies an independent and 'knowable' truth against which representations of it can be measured), but in terms of their usefulness in making sense of the world (which does not imply such a thing).

Of course, if we need to make sense of the world, then there must be a world to make sense of, and this world must present itself to us, or we must experience it, as something to make sense of. For this reason we do not simply appreciate and value Beckett's *Waiting for Godot*, if we do, because it is 'Beckettian,' but because we find in the Beckettian view of life something we consider to be 'true,' or at least to be 'more true' than some other views of life. Yet at the same time we do *not* believe that there is any independent and accessible 'truth about life' that can be used to check and corroborate the Beckettian version. If *Waiting for Godot* is an 'interpretative model' of human life, its relation to human life is not the same as the relation of a computer model of the earth's climate to the earth's actual climate. We cannot 'test' *Waiting for Godot* against any objective reality. In what sense, then, can it be considered 'true'?

Fictions cannot be true or false in the same sense that positive propositions (such as 'the earth's climate is getting warmer' or 'unemployment causes marital breakdowns') can be true or false. But this does not entail that they cannot reasonably be thought of being true or false in some sense. This point, however, is commonly misunderstood. If I utter a *simple* fictional sentence such as 'Once upon a time there was a very moody giant,' there is no question of its being true or false. It is neither true nor false, but fictional. But a play is not a *simple* fiction. It embodies some kind of 'internal logic' or consistency (which can be partly identified with the 'idea' or 'intention' behind it), and the question does arise of whether this is 'true to life' or not. This applies even in relation to a play such as Rozewicz's *Card Index*, which was discussed in Chapter Three. When we are confronted with a play such as this in which nothing seems 'true to life' in any superficial or conventional sense, and in which nothing even seems to make sense, then we must first identify what its 'internal logic' is. Suppose, simplistically, we say that its internal logic – what this play really dramatizes – is the *breakdown of all certainties*. Crudely, we then take this idea and ask if it is helpful in making sense of certain things in life and recent history. If we come to the conclusion that it helps us understand the experience of the Polish people in and after the Second World War, then we are ascribing to it a certain kind of truth.

It is notable in this context that the German marxist playwright Bertolt Brecht felt that he should write a play 'in answer' to Beckett's *Waiting for Godot*, although he died before he could do so. For Brecht, *Waiting for Godot* provided a false interpretative model of human life, but a persuasive one, hence worth contesting (which is a way of saying that Brecht thought Beckett had written a 'good' play). Since Brecht was a marxist who believed that theatre should have a political function, it is fairly obvious how his plays embody an internal logic which provides an interpretative model of human social existence. Moreover, up to a point we can say that a play by Brecht can be considered as being true or false in the same sense that marxism can be considered true or false – but only up to a point, for, in writing plays, Brecht understood that drama can communicate a different kind of truth than can political pamphlets. Dramatic form, in other words, is not just 'packaging,' but intrinsic and essential to the internal logic which is either true or false.

While clearly we need to think about how arts *in general* either do or do not embody and communicate knowledge, we should be careful not to lose sight of the essential differences between the arts. The kind of truth that can be captured in a play is different from the kind of truth that can be captured in a painting, precisely because these art forms work in different ways.

This point bears on another, perhaps even more difficult question. Can an art form such as drama be considered as a way of *finding something out*, as against a way of communicating something known?

Brecht's theory of the 'alienation effect' (*Verfremdungseffekt*), as discussed in Chapter Four, implies that the answer to this question is 'Yes'. At least, dramatic action can be presented in such a way as to cause the audience to think critically about the social reality to which the dramatic representation refers. In Brecht's project, the audience should not be allowed to become absorbed in the fiction, but encouraged to see past the fiction to the real world and at the same time to see this real world in a new light because of the way the fiction represents it.

One of the most 'Brechtian' of plays is not by Brecht himself. David Hare's *Fanshen* is set in rural China in the mid to late 1940s, at the time of the Revolution, and deals with land reform. The real subject of the drama, however, is *change*. Hare stresses that this is a play for a modern western audience with very little experience of real change. In production and performance a very subtle balance has to be struck between ensuring that the action seems authentic – since this is a true story of real historical events – and yet not letting the audience see it solely as a modern history play about other people in a very different social and political situation. On the contrary, the audience must be able to see in the rural Chinese example a kind of 'model' (not in the sense of an ideal, but of a tool for understanding) of the nature of change, one that provokes thought about what change is and how it might occur in the western world. This is achieved by what is ultimately Brecht's most valuable idea, the need for *simplification*. The whole style of the drama, conveyed in the way it is written, and the style of performance this calls for, focuses attention only on those elements of the action that really matter and excludes all over-characterization and excessive detail. This gives the action a kind of 'abstracted' quality which invites the audience, somewhat paradoxically, to see *more* in it than the representation of real history.

Brecht's work, at least from 1928 onwards, is really all directed at the same basic goal, that of presenting the world *as changeable*. Drama is a means through which the world can be discovered to be changeable, not one in which the audience is simply told that this is so. As we saw earlier in Chapter Four, however, this does not always work; at least, Brecht complained about the way critics misunderstood *Mother Courage and her Children*. Still, such misunderstanding may reflect the ideological predisposition of the critics more than it does any weakness in Brecht's ideas about theatre. Nonetheless, according to the Brazilian theatre worker Augusto Boal, if the goal is to bring the spectator to the point of discovering that the world really is changeable, then it is necessary to go an important step further than Brecht did.

Boal's approach to theatre can be summed up in the idea that *'spectator' is a bad word*. Instead, he proposes the concept of the *spectactor*, a word coined by fusing together 'spectator' and 'actor'. A spectactor is a spectator who is able to intervene in the action of the play and to change it in some way. The concept grew from Boal's early practice of 'simultaneous playwrighting' in which spectators were presented with a dramatized problem and asked to propose solutions to it which the actors would then test by acting them out. He then found that it was better to allow spectators not only to propose solutions or alternative ways of doing something, but actually to get up on stage, take over a role and put their ideas into practice themselves. This practice is now referred to as Forum Theatre. In Forum Theatre, the initial play models some social situation of relevance to the audience, such as the refusal of certain welfare benefits to a single mother. The play is short – because it needs to be played more than once – and ends badly for the protagonist. During the second run-through, the audience is able to intervene by suggesting and trying out alternative strategies which may help the protagonist and even bring about a 'happy ending'. However, this must not happen 'magically'. It is up to the spectators collectively, as well as the actors and a facilitator called the 'Joker,' to make sure that the play really does continue to model the real-life situation it is about.

Forum Theatre really works on two levels. The solutions that are found to a particular problem, as this problem is dramatized in the initial play, should be practical and realistic. Beyond this, the experience of participation reveals the more general truth that the world is changeable. This second level, of course, rests on the first. The difficult 'TOK' question (or problem of knowledge) that arises here is, how is it decided whether proposed solutions are 'practical and realistic' or not? Is it the case that trying out such solutions in a dramatic imitation of life is more effective as a test than simple debate?

It is not enough, Boal implies, for plays to model life. If it were, a play could simply present solutions to its audience. Rather, the *truth* of the model has to be discovered through the *process* of modelling. This relates to what (in modern educational jargon) can be called the 'ownership' of knowledge. There are things that we can 'know' in a weak sense, but unless we 'own this knowledge,' we do not really or fully know them. In other words, what we discover for ourselves is more important and valuable as knowledge than what we are told (at least where both options are open).

Note, then, that Forum Theatre does not produce *literature*, although it is drama. From Boal's point of view, literature is too 'fixed' to be a way of knowing. More generally as far as literature is concerned, the question is this: in reading, to what extent does the reader discover things for herself or himself and to what extent is s/he told things?

APPENDIX
TRAGEDY, COMEDY AND TRAGICOMEDY

The theatre is often symbolized by a pair of masks, one expressing grief and the other laughter. These masks represent tragedy and comedy. Of course, not all plays fit neatly in one or the other category. But in their polarity, or opposition, tragedy and comedy still define the *range* of theatrical experience.

The distinction goes back to the fifth century BCE when a dramatic competition was held in Athens during the springtime festival, called the Greater or City Dionysia, in honour of the god Dionysos. Prizes were given both for the best tragedy (from about 530 BCE) and the best comedy (from 486 BCE). It is arguable that tragedy and comedy represented the two sides – one terrifying, the other joyful – of the god. However, the extant Greek tragedies do not all seem to be 'tragedies' in the modern understanding of the term, although a great deal of suffering occurs in many of them. Tragedy at that time was more or less synonymous with 'serious drama'. Today, it is still common to distinguish between drama and comedy, in the sense of the term 'drama' that implies action with a certain quality to grip or move the audience. Moreover, we have come to think of tragedy as an especially intense kind of drama which follows certain basic principles. To understand more fully what these principles are, it helps to take a historical overview.

TRAGEDY

In everyday life, we use the terms 'tragedy' or 'tragic' to describe unfortunate events which involve suffering, injury or loss of life. Tragedy in the theatre is more strictly defined. Although misfortune and suffering are essential here too, a merely accidental calamity does not amount to a true tragedy. This implies that it is not suffering in itself that matters. Rather, when we read or watch a theatrical tragedy, we are confronted with difficult questions about the nature of human existence. Above all, we are asked to consider the relationship between our own responsibility for the consequences of our actions and the cruel or indifferent universe in which we live. The first to provide some useful insights into how tragedy does this was Aristotle.

In his *Poetics*, written about a century after the great age of Attic tragedy, Aristotle defines tragedy as an imitation (*mimesis*) of action, in dramatic form, whose plot arouses pity and fear in the spectator. We pity the tragic hero because the fate that befalls him or her seems worse than any fault on his or her part deserves. Given that we can identify with the hero, we also fear that something similar might happen to us. But this is not all. According to Aristotle, tragedy also accomplishes the *catharsis* of the emotions of pity and fear. Literally translated, catharsis means 'cleansing' or 'purgation' or 'purification'. Catharsis occurs insofar as we do not experience pity and fear as unpleasant emotions and we do not continue to feel them after the play is over.

Aristotle considers plot of primary importance in tragedy. He argues that a good tragic plot should involve a reversal of fortune (*peripeteia*) or a recognition (*anagnorisis*) or both. Both of these involve change. A discovery is a change from ignorance to knowledge. A reversal is either a change from good to bad fortune or a change from bad to good fortune. It seems strange to us that the latter should be counted 'tragic,' but Aristotle accepts this, although he also argues that the best tragic plots see the hero go from good to bad fortune. The reason concerns the earlier argument that tragedies should arouse pity and fear in the spectator, since neither of these is likely to arise as we watch someone's situation getting better. Moreover, not only should the reversal be from good to bad fortune, but, most importantly, a specific kind of tragic hero is necessary if pity and fear are to be aroused.

Suppose we see a wholly good man pass from happiness to misery. According to Aristotle, this is not truly fear-inspiring, nor does it evoke pity. Rather, it appalls us as too unjust. If, alternatively, we were to see a very bad man pass from happiness to misery, we would simply feel that this is what he deserves. If, instead, such a bad man were to go from bad to good fortune, Aristotle seems to imply that we would have no significant feelings about it at all. All three of these plots are to be avoided. As for the case of a wholly good man who goes from bad to good fortune, Aristotle does not comment directly on it. What then is left? Clearly, we should stop thinking in terms of 'wholly good' or 'wholly bad' heroes. Instead, the tragic hero should be *good but not wholly good*, for this is the kind of person with whom we can most easily identify. ('Good but not wholly good' is, by implication, how we tend to think of ourselves.) Moreover, when such a person passes from good to bad fortune, he should do so not in consequence of random chance but because of his own fault or weakness or error of judgment (*hamartia*). Where this occurs, great misfortune is strictly *undeserved*, hence it is to be pitied. This would not be the case if it were caused by some depravity. At the same time, our sense of justice is not wholly violated, since the reversal of fortune was caused by some error on the hero's part.

Aristotle's conception of the tragic hero is very useful, but it is obvious that it applies to certain characters such as the serial killer Macbeth only if it is interpreted with subtlety! Most importantly, it points us to what seems to be a kind of key to tragedy: the tragic hero is responsible for his or her own misfortune and suffering, but that misfortune and suffering are nonetheless greater than deserved.

In Europe, the rise of Christianity meant that for many centuries no significant drama was produced. During this time there certainly existed bands of travelling players performing popular entertainments of various kinds, amongst which there may well have been dramatic imitations, but the attitude of the Christian church was initially hostile to theatre. Christians were forbidden to attend performances or participate in them. Nonetheless, by the later middle ages two significant forms of drama had emerged, both Christian in inspiration. These were Mystery plays, which enacted Bible stories, and Morality plays, which were allegories of virtue and vice. As these forms developed, more and more comic elements were incorporated into them (such as the characterization of Noah's wife as a nagging 'shrew'), sometimes to reinforce the Christian message but often purely for entertainment. They cannot be called 'comedies,' however. Nor are they 'tragedies' in any sense.

What really matters here is that *Christian theology is incompatible with a truly tragic view of life.* (The Greek sense of tragedy, in contrast, had emerged from the heroic ethos as expressed in *The Iliad.*) To a good Christian, sufferings in this life do not ultimately matter; indeed, they are sometimes actively sought! What matters is the afterlife. Moreover, since God is just, there is no question of someone suffering, at least in the afterlife, 'more than s/he deserves'. Christian writers such as Chaucer may still use the word 'tragedy,' but what they mean by it is little more than a 'moral lesson'; that is, since the wheel of fortune can always turn against you, you should not count on worldly success or goods or happiness, but focus on the life to come.

The re-birth of tragedy on the Elizabethan and Jacobean[1] stage rests ultimately on a revaluation of our earthly life as something more than a prelude and a test and thus it rests on the demise of the medieval world view. It was triggered, however, by the influence of ancient plays, in particular the tragedies of the Roman dramatist, Seneca. Seneca lived nearly five hundred years after Aeschylus, Sophocles and Euripides, but his tragedies were largely modeled on those of classical Greece and he even used the same legends and myths for his plots. The discovery and translation of his plays in Tudor England (following their publication in Italy in 1474) led to their imitation by native writers. Soon such imitations became mixed with elements from native, popular theatrical tradition. Here began that synthesis of 'grand, poetic style,' taken over from Seneca, and theatrical pace and flexibility, learnt in the popular theatre, which leads straight to Shakespeare.

The first native English tragedy was *Gorboduc*, written by two lawyers in 1561, Thomas Norton and Thomas Sackville. It is a studied and stilted imitation of Senecan style with little sense of drama as action or entertainment. By the 1580s, however, a new kind of 'semi-professional' playwright was emerging, whose livelihood depended, at least in part, on the proverbial 'bums on seats'. Unlike Norton and Sackville, and unlike Seneca himself (who wrote for his friends), they had a public to please. The crucial step was *to put as much as possible of the real action of the story onstage.* Seneca, following the Greek conventions, had left violent acts (with which his stories are filled) to the imagination, locating them offstage and relying on the power of words to evoke their image. Elizabethan playwrights realized that this was not 'good box office'. The first English dramatist successfully to combine an elevated style with gripping, fast-moving and at times gory onstage action was probably Thomas Kyd in *The Spanish Tragedy*, although the exact date of this play is unknown (it was written at some time between 1582 and 1592). Hence Kyd has become known as the 'father of English tragedy'.

Some of the tragic heroes of this period, such as Othello, seem quite clearly to meet the Aristotelian template of a man who is 'good but not wholly good'. But many do not, at least not in a straightforward way. Yet it tends to remain the case, firstly, that the tragic hero is responsible for his fall and, secondly, that his fall is worse than he deserves, thus arousing the emotions of pity and fear. The most significant difference from the Greek model lies in the fact that the Elizabethan or Jacobean tragic fall is often not a simple or momentary reversal of fortune that comes as a climax to the action, but an extended decline including a moral decline. Thus to see Macbeth's fall as worse than he deserves, we must interpret it as including the moral degeneration that begins from the moment he consents to kill Duncan. This way of looking at things helps us see Marlowe's Dr Faustus as a tragic hero, too, although by

---

[1] The term 'Jacobean' refers to the reign of James I in England from 1603 to 1627. Elizabeth I reigned from 1558 to 1603.

definition in the context of Christian theology his final punishment by God cannot be 'worse than he deserves'. Even the villainous Daniel de Bossola in Webster's *The Duchess of Malfi* is a tragic hero in this sense, one whose fall has effectively happened before the start of the play! (See Chapter Two for some analysis of Bossola's very complex character.)

The status of tragedy in the modern world is problematic. The late nineteenth century saw the rise of naturalism and with it the dominance of *domestic drama*, although the latter had first emerged in the eighteenth century. Domestic drama focuses on the middle classes. Traditionally, the heroes of tragedy are high born. This is not for the crude reason that those who are highest up the social scale have furthest to fall, but because tragedy deals with 'higher things'. The assumption made by earlier tragedians is that lower class characters have little or no relation to these 'higher things'. Now, the phrase 'higher things' is very vague. What it means is, firstly, that events in tragedy exceed the normal – for tragedy deals with extremes – and, secondly, more importantly, that tragic action concerns the relationship of human beings to the broader cosmos – perhaps to the gods, or to metaphysical forces, perhaps to something more like the law of *karma* – rather than their social relationships to each other (the latter being more the material of comedy). Lower class characters, in the traditional approach, lead intrinsically 'normal' lives and are defined entirely in terms of their social position and social relations. Thus the tragic dimension of life is beyond them.

To us, such an attitude seems purely prejudiced. Why should a lower class character not be a tragic hero? However, we also need to acknowledge that as the middle classes became socially dominant, they tended to establish a new world view in which human life and experience is seen as largely determined by social rather than cosmic forces. For this reason, domestic drama has a rather ambiguous relationship to tragedy.

August Strindberg's *Miss Julie* is especially relevant in this context, since it is about the decline of aristocratic values, represented by Miss Julie herself, and the attendant rise of a bourgeois mentality, represented by the valet, Jean. The fall of Miss Julie is not only 'tragic' – it is a kind of 'meta-tragedy,' the tragedy of the end of tragedy. This is why, in his important Preface, Strindberg makes the apparently strange remark that the audience should blame itself, not the playwright, if it finds his tragedy too tragic! The class values of a character like Miss Julie no longer have survival value, Strindberg implies, and there is no point in feeling pity, let alone fear, at their demise. The emerging world belongs to the likes of Jean. We may recognize that, for all his superficial refinement and for all the qualities that make him stronger than Miss Julie, he – and the class he represents – is fundamentally mean-spirited, but we should no more lament her fall and his rise than we should the colonization of a biological niche by a new and better adapted species.

Strindberg's argument points to a real problem. *Social forces*, which cause the rise and fall of classes, are not inherently tragic. This is a point that Bertolt Brecht was later to elaborate. Social forces are not god-sent or god-given; they may determine the lives of many, even most, but they are themselves the product of human activity and as such they are subject to human intervention. In other words, it is possible to change the world. The way the world actually is involves huge injustice and great suffering, but to conceive this as 'tragic' – at least in the strong sense of the term – is to accept it as the inevitable consequence of human limitation. It is to confuse the political with the metaphysical. To fight against it, to seek to change things, on the other hand, *can never be tragic,* for it entails that the story is not yet over. (See Chapter Four for some discussion of how Brecht's *Mother Courage and her Children* was mistaken as a tragedy by the 'bourgeois press'.)

In the twentieth century, the social status of many central characters was reduced even further. In tandem with this, and perhaps related to it, relatively few twentieth century plays count as true tragedies. It may even be the case that a future assessment of the major drama of the twentieth century will see the period as 'a great age of tragicomedy'.

A play that represents the 'problem' of tragedy in the twentieth century is Arthur Miller's *Death of a Salesman*. Willy Loman's low status is underlined by his name (Loman = low man), a name which also hints that he is a kind of 'Everyman' figure. The play charts the last stages of Willy's failure in life, a failure that is partly objective, an economic fact, and partly subjective, a sense of failure. But although Willy clearly falls, the problem of whether or not *Death of a Salesman* can be called a tragedy concerns the degree of responsibility its hero has for his own fate. If Willy can be thought of as having 'freely chosen' the illusions of the 'American Dream,' then his fall (that is, his failure) follows from this 'error of judgment' as, in a good tragedy, it should. Certainly, Willy is seen as being *instrumental* in his own dreams and illusions, at least in the way he actively tries to sustain them. If this were not so, there would be no point in his son, Biff, trying to make him face up to reality. However, this is not to say that he is *responsible*, for it is not to say that he freely 'bought into' the dream *in the first place*. In fact he seems to be much more a victim of the American Dream than a man who reaps the consequences of his own individual error, and this seems to be a precondition of his implicit status as an Everyman figure. Insofar as he is ultimately *nothing more than a victim,* he is not a true tragic hero, for he has no ultimate responsibility for his fate. Moreover, he is the victim merely of (changeable) social forces.

However, certain twentieth century playwrights, in particular Frederico Garcia Lorca and Jean Anouilh, believed that tragedy remained viable and relevant in the modern age. Lorca consciously tried to write tragedies in which events occur with an inescapable necessity, that is, where the tragic outcome seems *fated*. Thus, when the newly married Bride runs away with Leonardo in *Blood Wedding*, it is not because of a reckless impulse or deliberate choice, but because she experiences some deep, incomprehensible and irresistible compulsion. We can psychologize this if we will, by calling it 'obsession,' but it is strongly reminiscent of the 'daemonic possession' that drives certain ancient Greek tragedies such as Aeschylus' *Agamemnon* and Euripides' *Medea*.

Moreover, while Lorca locates one source of the tragedy in the social world, which he presents as narrow and restricted, especially for women, he constructs the play so as to leave that social world behind once the social restriction is broken, for he understood that true tragedy takes us beyond our merely social being. Hence, in a remarkable experiment with form, the realism of the first two acts is discarded and a dreamlike world of elemental, metaphysical powers is put on stage. Through this we see that, for Lorca, society is not self-contained and autonomous, but a part of a wider (or deeper) reality comprising heat, blood, passion and the dark sources of poetry.

There is another way in which *Blood Wedding* echoes or recreates the original sense of tragedy of ancient Greece (as distinct from Aristotle's later rationalization of it) – its very close association with lament. Not only does Lorca's play end with formal lamentation, as do several Greek tragedies, but the bitter spirit of lament informs it from the beginning. Through the Mother's inability to accept the violent deaths of her husband and first-born son, we know we are in a tragic world from the start, not in the 'normal' modern world in which sometimes things happen to go – 'tragically' – wrong.

Anouilh too associated tragedy with fate. The Chorus in his *Antigone* explicitly comments on the way in which, in tragedy, one thing leads to another with an inescapable, machine-like logic. But while an inevitably tragic outcome is built into the situation, it takes a kind of 'free choice' *to be a tragic heroine* on Antigone's own part to set the wheels of tragedy in motion. In fact, Anouilh's Antigone knowingly *chooses* tragedy in a way that most tragic figures do not. Her choice is not like the compulsion that drives Lorca's Bride, which is a desire for something other than tragedy itself, even as she must know the inevitable tragic outcome of her decision to run away with Leonardo. In Antigone, in fact, 'fate' is really built into Creon's situation as king. He first tries to cover up the crime itself, then, when Antigone is discovered as the perpetrator, he tries to hide this fact too. But Antigone *obliges* him to act as his position and duty as king *oblige* him to act, by punishing her. In this sense, the willful heroine both exploits and brings out something *given* in the situation. Once she does this, the tragedy truly begins.

COMEDY

Broadly speaking, comedy is defined in relation to two things, firstly the way it arouses amusement or laughter in the audience and secondly the way it tends to end happily. But, apart from this general rule, comedy is much more open to variation than is tragedy. In fact, many different kinds of comedy have evolved. Several of these are defined in the Glossary.

There are four principal sources of humour in plays: 1) comic characters with certain exaggerated characteristics – often these are types such as the Fop, the Pedant, the Old Man with a young wife, the Miser or the Cunning Servant; 2) the plot, as this generates contrived and complicated situations, quite commonly involving mistaken identities; 3) the dialogue, as it contains witty remarks and epigrams, puns and other wordplay, innuendo, malapropisms, pomposity and such like; and 4) visual gags, such as clowning routines and slapstick. A comic play usually contains some mix of these, though one or other may be predominant depending on the type of comedy it is. Notably, comedies where the focus of interest is the plot can still take 'time out' from plot development to include other sorts of humour and often contain certain 'inessential' characters for this purpose.

Comedy makes us laugh, but laughter is not an emotion in the way that pity and fear are emotions. It is a physiological response, involving rhythmic, explosive convulsions of the abdomen, diaphragm and vocal organs resulting in repetitious, inarticulate noise. It can express a range of emotions from joy to scorn. Strangely, it is infectious; we can start laughing for no other reason than that someone else is laughing. It is also healthy. A 'good laugh' makes us feel better and may even prolong life. It is easy enough to understand why we enjoy laughter but much more difficult to say what the *significance* of our laughter is. This becomes a problem where we have to write about comedies in the theatre.

Quite commonly, a distinction is made between laughing *at* and laughing *with* a person. We tend to laugh at people when they appear ridiculous or foolish. We laugh with them when in some way they draw our attention to the existence of some kind of absurdity. This distinction is certainly useful in relation to plays. In Dario Fo's *Accidental Death of an Anarchist*, for example, we laugh with the Maniac but at the police, precisely because they are made to look so foolish by the Maniac. For much of Ben Jonson's *Volpone*, we laugh with Volpone and his 'parasite' Mosca, even though these characters are vicious, as they deceive and prey on a series of foolish characters, at whom we can only laugh.

Laughing 'with' implies a certain sympathy or common point of view. Laughing 'at' may be cruel, but it is not necessarily cruel. This is not only because a character may deserve to be laughed at, but also because we can be induced to feel a kind of affection for some kinds of 'ridiculous' or 'foolish' characters, at least in the fictional world of a play. Lady Bracknell, in Oscar Wilde's *The Importance of Being Earnest,* is domineering, smug and materialistic, but the pleasure we gain from the laughter she provokes generates a kind of 'liking' for her. This is because we do not exactly laugh at the fact that she is domineering or materialistic. We laugh at certain *exaggerations* in her character, together with the absurdity of much that she says, which also happen to draw our attention to these negative features.

Moreover, laughing 'at' a character may not be cruel for another reason. When a person 'slips on a banana skin' and falls, others may laugh – but they only do so insofar as no injury occurs. What is funny in a case like this is not another's pain but rather the slipping of the conventional, respectable social mask, in this case the dignity of upright posture, just as it is in the other cliché comic situation where someone's trousers fall down in public. When this mask slips, it is seen to be a mask, but no harm is done. Comedy, in this sense, is *inconsequential*. This fact is closely related to the association of comedy with the happy ending. Things can and do go wrong in comedies, but they don't go seriously wrong.

The world of comedy is fundamentally different from the world of tragedy. The fundamental premise of tragedy is that human beings must accept responsibility for their actions and for the consequences of their actions, even where these consequences are disproportionate to the degree of fault in the original action. The fundamental premise of comedy, on the other hand, is that human beings are only held responsible for their actions, if they are, by other human beings, and only when the worst consequences of these actions have been successfully avoided. In effect, such characters are held responsible for their intentions.

The so-called Comedy of Vice and Folly illustrates this principle most clearly. Both vicious and foolish actions can lead to bad consequences. Vicious characters intend such consequences, however, while foolish characters do not. As the action is resolved, the bad – or at least the worst – consequences of earlier actions are avoided. Nevertheless, intention itself must be appropriately dealt with. Hence vicious characters, like Moliere's Tartuffe or Jonson's Volpone, are punished, usually by the law or other social authority. Foolish characters, in contrast, are merely exposed as the fools that they are (though the fools in *Volpone* have vicious streaks and are punished accordingly). In tragedy, quite differently, it is never intention that is 'punished,' but action, and that not by merely human authority.

Not all comedies include vicious characters, of course. Nonetheless a certain theory of comedy, which goes back to Aristotle, attributes a kind of *moral purpose* to it. Aristotle remarks that comedy imitates men who are 'worse than the average' in the sense that they are ridiculous. The ridiculous, he says, is a kind of ugliness (just as the traditional comic mask is ugly), but it is not harmful of others. Though Aristotle does not say so, it is reasonable to infer from this that the moral point of comedy lies in the *exposure* of the ridiculous.

In his Preface to his novel *Joseph Andrews*, Henry Fielding provides an excellent elaboration of this idea. The truly ridiculous is only *affectation*, he asserts, and affectation has just two sources: vanity and hypocrisy. *Vanity* is a kind of self-deceit, while *hypocrisy* involves deceiving others. The pleasure of comedy lies in the way it restores the truth by exposing affectation for what it is. Note then that affectation is exposed to the audience, allowing them to laugh at it, before it is exposed to other characters, for very often the latter only occurs in the resolution of the plot. When, prior to this, we laugh at what we know to be affectation, we do so in the knowledge that it will be exposed to others in the play at a later stage. It is important that this happens. It is also important to understand that *exposure is a social fate*, for comedy is more concerned with the nature of our social life than is tragedy.

Such a theory attributes a clear moral purpose to comedy. There are, however, two problems with it. The first problem concerns the type of comedy that Fielding has in mind, for it is not always as simple as Fielding implies, while the second problem is just that not all comedy is of this type. To understand comedy more fully, then, we need to consider both problems in more detail.

In the first place, comedy that appears to have the moral purpose of exposing affectation is sometimes morally ambivalent, or at least much more complex morally than Fielding suggests. This is especially true where the comic dramatist's target is not so much certain individuals or types but the *society* in which they exist, that is, where individual affectation is symptomatic of a wider social malaise. Widespread affectation allows certain unscrupulous but unaffected characters to prey on others or at least to scheme successfully to get what they want. Such characters, 'immoral' though they are, very often engage our sympathies at least up to a point and for a time, both because they are not affected themselves and because they know that other characters are affected. Where this is the case, the overall 'feel' of the play is usually satirical.

A fine example of this is William Wycherley's *The Country Wife*. In this Restoration Comedy (a type of comedy that gave rise to eighteenth-century Comedy of Manners), the unscrupulous but unaffected character is Horner, a rake or libertine whose goal is to seduce married women and to cuckold their husbands. The two husbands seen in the play, the gullible Sir Jasper and the grotesquely jealous Mr Pinchwife, both seem to deserve to be cuckolded, for this is made to appear not only as a 'punishment' for their foolishness but as an almost 'inevitable' consequence of it! Moreover, Horner knows and understands the world – an understanding expressed both in his witty observations and his ability to dupe others. Through his stratagems (he pretends to be impotent in order to gain access to other men's wives), he exposes sham and hypocrisy, especially the concern for reputation. That may not be *his* main motive (if it is Wycherley's), but he clearly enjoys this aspect of the game he plays. Indeed, he has no sentimental or emotional involvement with the women he seduces and his goal is probably more to pull off the trick than it is sexual gratification. His enjoyment in this coincides with our enjoyment in seeing affectation exposed and certain kinds of folly 'punished' (note, in relation to this, that being cuckolded is a 'punishment' only because the cuckolded characters consider it to be a terrible thing to happen to them).

Moreover, Wycherley does little to counterbalance the amorality of his rake-hero, Horner, with more conventionally moral characters. The closest to the latter is Alithea, who for a long time refuses the advances of Harcourt because she is engaged to Sparkish. It is revealed, however, that the reason for her fidelity is that Sparkish seems to lack jealousy; she wishes to remain in London and to enjoy its liberties, whereas a jealous husband would probably remove her to the country. Harcourt himself begins as a rake, but, genuinely falling in love with Alithea (at least insofar as such a thing is possible in Restoration Comedy), he is content in the end to marry. But Wycherley does not develop the character or this plot line to the extent necessary for Harcourt to be a genuine alternative to Horner. Instead, the playwright's intention is to expose the faults of the world through the 'Nemesis figure,' Horner himself, that such a world deserves.

It is instructive to compare this with a comedy that conforms to Fielding's prescription much more closely. Richard Sheridan's Comedy of Manners, *The School for Scandal,* also depicts a kind of social malaise in the form of widespread gossip, backbiting, slander and general scandal mongering – as neatly suggested in the names of characters such as Lady Sneerwell and Sir Benjamin Backbite. In this case, however, the comedy's moral purpose is fulfilled and hypocrisy is exposed without generating any moral ambivalence. This is largely because Sheridan builds in a character, Sir Oliver Surface, from beyond the social world depicted in the play (he has been abroad for fifteen years), who is able to see through the 'masks' of reputation from his first appearance in Act 2, Scene 3. It is largely Sir Oliver who devises means to expose the truth. Horner, in contrast, is a product of the world he serves to expose. But precisely because Sheridan's play contains and relies on a morally just outsider, it does not *fully dramatize* the world it satirizes. That is, it does not allow the logic of that world to work itself out in its own terms, but transforms it by means of a kind of 'good angel'. For this reason, the satire becomes somewhat detached from the working out of the comic plot and to that extent it is undermined as the play progresses, becoming replaced by a more reassuring and 'comfortable' view of the world. This suggests, perhaps, that the kind of comedy that best fits Fielding's conception may be – at least to modern taste – too 'easy'.

The second problem with Fielding's conception of the moral purpose of comedy lies in the fact that laughter arises from many things other than the exposure of affectation. Some of these other things might also be classed as 'ridiculous,' such that we laugh *at* them, but others are such that we laugh *with* them. Moreover, the distinction between laughing at and laughing with is itself much more subtle than is often suggested. A good clowning routine, for example, often generates a complex mixture of laughter at and laughter with the clown.

To understand this more fully, we need to see that comedy often involves *the breakdown and subversion of conventional norms*. So too does tragedy, of course, but comic *disorder* is typically enjoyable for its own sake. It is understood that order must and will be restored in the end, but for the interim something akin to the 'spirit of carnival' rules as conventional propriety, social restraints and established hierarchy are overturned.

To a great extent we can associate this side of comedy with the so-called Old Comedy of ancient Athens, represented for us by nine of the eleven surviving plays of Aristophanes. The more obviously moralistic type of comedy, on the other hand, originated in the New Comedy of Menander in Greece and of Plautus and Terence in Rome. Old Comedy can have a moral purpose, one which is manifested at the level of its plot; *Lysistrata*, to take an obvious example, is intended to reveal the folly of the Peloponnesian War (already in its twentieth year in 411 BCE, when Aristophanes' play was first produced). But while New Comedy and its descendants tend to reestablish or reassert *existing* social norms, or rather the ideal versions of them, in their resolutions, *Lysistrata* offers the then unthinkable and entirely subversive image of women taking control of politics. Old Comedy is often *utopian* in this way. But quite apart from any overall 'message' conveyed by the plot, Old Comedy is subversive in its frank relish of sex and sensuality, its 'zany' imagination and disregard of all realism, and its sheer spirit of fun.

Of course, it is questionable just how subversive this kind of comedy really is; arguably, it functions more as a kind of safety valve for suppressed instincts, just as carnival itself does. However, this question cannot be answered in the abstract, for it depends on the degree of tolerance of the society in which such plays are produced. It is often assumed, in fact, that Old Comedy died out in Athens because it became politically unacceptable.

Subversive, carnivalesque Old Comedy is relatively rare in the literary tradition, at least after Aristophanes, but elements or aspects of it can be found in other sorts of written comedy. It is as though its anarchic spirit is always under the surface waiting to break through and disrupt normality. It is arguable, moreover, that Romantic Comedy embodies a reduced or 'watered down' version of this subversive spirit, especially in its utopianism. In Romantic Comedy, young lovers are often kept apart by an older figure of *authority*, usually a father. In the obligatory happy ending, the resistance of the older man is overcome and the lovers are united. In fact, according to Northrop Frye, comedy enacts the victory of Youth over Age (not only in Romantic Comedy, but also in other types where older characters are figures of fun). It enacts in this way an overthrow of the existing order and its replacement by a new one. Moreover, we see in a Romantic Comedy like Shakespeare's *A Midsummer Night's Dream* not just the victory of Youth over Age, but a phase of the action in which the existing social order is temporarily left behind (which is not the same as its overthrow, of course) and a different, in some ways 'dangerous' but also strangely 'liberating' world is encountered, the forest at night, a world whose essential nature is embodied in the very spirit of mischief, Puck. Nonetheless, the obligatory resolution of Romantic Comedy – marriage, or at least the promise of it – is a restoration of social order. In fact, comedies nearly always end not just happily but with a kind of *overcoming* of or *leaving behind* the disruptive spirit of fun itself.

TRAGICOMEDY

We have seen that the 'worlds' of tragedy and comedy are very different. Yet it is possible to combine or mix these worlds.

Some of Shakespeare's tragedies contain scenes of so-called 'comic relief,' such as the Grave Diggers scene (5,1) in *Hamlet*. Whether such scenes really provide 'relief' from the tensions of tragedy is debatable, but they certainly provide an alternative perspective and a reminder that, even in tragedy, there are those who live in a non-tragic world. However, the important point here is that such scenes, though comic in themselves, do not shift the play towards comedy. We remain wholly aware that we are watching a tragedy.

A 'problem play' such as Shakespeare's *Measure for Measure* is more relevant here. Watching or reading this play we have the sense that, up until the middle of Act 4, it *might have been a tragedy,* although from this point onwards it becomes more unambiguously a comedy. It might have been a tragedy, moreover, in spite of the fact that a number of earlier scenes make us laugh. It is as though the action raises issues and questions that are 'too serious' for comedy. That action, moreover, leads to what might easily have become a catastrophe. The character of Angelo, too, is necessarily more complex than we would expect in a comedy. Yet, for all this, we cannot call *Measure for Measure* a tragicomedy, at least in the modern sense of this term, for its resolution clearly identifies it as a comedy, albeit a highly problematic one.

The modern sense of tragicomedy originates with the work of Chekhov. It is notable that Chekhov himself thought of two of his major plays, *The Seagull* and *The Cherry Orchard*, as comedies whereas Stanislavski, who directed them at the Moscow Arts Theatre, interpreted them as tragedies. There is no point here in asking who was 'right'. What matters is that such a divergence of opinion could have arisen in the first place. It implies that these plays generate a kind of ambivalence. We do not know whether to pity the characters or to laugh at them, for both responses seem equally appropriate. But why should this be?

We can answer this question in terms of *the degree and kind of responsibility that characters bear for the situations they are in*. In tragedy, the hero is responsible for his fate, at least up to some point. That fate is the ultimate consequence of some error. However, once the error has been made, the tragic fate that follows from it is inevitable and can be 'known in advance,' as Anouilh's Chorus points out in *Antigone*. There is no turning back, no escaping the consequences of one's actions, as there is in comedy. In tragicomedy, on the other hand, the hero (often an inappropriate word in this context) – and other characters – may be in a pitiful situation, a situation at least partly of their own making, *but it is not inevitable*. Their responsibility for their present situation, thus, is a *present responsibility*, not a past responsibility. That is, it is still open to them to change their situation, at least for much of the play. They suffer, but they do not have to suffer. Now, this kind of responsibility is a kind of foolishness, hence we can laugh at it even as we are aware that it is piteous, a source of suffering. However, we must be careful not to oversimplify this point, for tragicomedy is often very subtle in its effects. Madame Ranyevskaia, in *The Cherry Orchard,* could, if she chose to, follow Lopakhin's advice and lease the orchard land for holiday villas. She could, if she chose to, accept the onward march of history and 'progress'. To the extent that she does not do so, she is responsible for her own fate. But we are made aware at the very same time that Ranyevskaia would not be Ranyevskaia if she behaved like this. In this sense, then, she both can and cannot change her fate. We laugh insofar as she can and cry insofar as she cannot.

Samuel Beckett develops precisely this sense of tragicomedy in many of his plays. Beckett's suffering characters seem to exemplify the 'human condition' as largely defined by inevitable decline and death, but they are also in large part *the architects of their own worlds*. In fact Beckett's most famous play, *Waiting for Godot,* enacts precisely a 'drama of responsibility' which can be taken as exemplary of tragicomedy. What Vladimir and Estragon 'do' throughout the play is wait, but their motive in this is that they expect Godot, for whom they wait, to take responsibility for their lives by telling them what to do. Godot does not come. What we witness, then, is the ironic situation in which the two *continue* to be responsible for their lives as they choose to go on waiting, that is, trying or hoping to *cease* or *give up* being responsible for their lives! Yet, in the way we put this, we must be careful not to make it seem mere foolishness, for it is not clear what else they might do.

We can sum all this up simply by repeating and extending something said earlier. The fundamental premise of tragedy is that human beings must accept responsibility for their actions and for the consequences of their actions, even where these consequences are disproportionate to the degree of fault in the original action. The fundamental premise of comedy is that human beings are only held responsible for their actions, if they are, by other human beings, and only when the worst consequences of these actions have been successfully avoided. Lastly, the fundamental premise of (modern) tragicomedy is that human beings are seen to be responsible for their piteous situations or fates, but in an ongoing or 'continuously chosen' way that is foolish insofar as it is not inevitable but not foolish insofar as it lacks any viable or practical or credible alternative.

GLOSSARY OF TERMS
RELATED TO DRAMA AND THEATRE

ABSURDISM (THEATRE OF THE ABSURD) A post World War II style of theatre associated above all with Samuel Beckett and Eugene Ionesco in which human existence is presented in a non-naturalistic way as if it makes no sense and has no point. In Absurdist Theatre, the relative certainties of tragedy and traditional comedy break down, resulting in tragicomedy or in new, surreal kinds of comedy. Absurdism influenced dramatists such as Albee, Havel and Pinter.

ACT A major segment of a play. An act may be a continuous single scene or a sequence of discontinuous scenes. Also, what an actor does.

ACTION Something done by a character which is aimed at achieving a specific goal and which advances the plot. More generally, the principal events that make up the plot.

ACTIVITY Something done by a character in a play which does not advance the plot.

ACTOR One who impersonates a character in a dramatic fiction.

ALIENATION EFFECT A concept introduced by Bertolt Brecht whereby the attention of the audience is drawn to the artifice of theatrical presentation in order to prevent the audience identifying too closely with a character and to encourage it to think about the social reality which is being represented. Also but less often called 'distanciation' or 'estrangement'.

ANAGNORISIS Recognition or discovery, a change from ignorance to knowledge. According to Aristotle, a feature of tragedy, but common in comedy too.

ANTAGONIST The principal adversary of the protagonist in a conflict between them.

APRON STAGE A playing space with the audience on three sides. The same as a thrust stage.

ARENA STAGE A playing space with the audience on four sides or arranged in a circle around it. The same as theatre in the round.

ASIDE Line or lines spoken by a character and understood by convention not to be heard by some or all of the other characters then onstage.

AUDIENCE PARTICIPATION Anything required from the audience, or from certain members of it, over and above its attention, which counts as part of the show.

AUDITORIUM The part of an indoor theatre in which the audience sits or stands.

BLACK BOX A small-scale theatre venue consisting of a room in which the seating arrangement of the audience and hence the playing space itself can be varied to suit the needs of the play or production.

BLACKOUT Complete darkness on stage. Abrupt transition from a lit stage to an unlit one.

BOX SET A stage set complete with walls which represents a room.

BUSINESS Something done by an actor when in character but which is incidental to the main action, such as serving coffee or reading a magazine. Similar to activity.

CAST The actors selected to play the parts in a play. As a verb, to choose an actor for a part.

CATASTROPHE Literally an overturning or overthrowing, a disastrous or calamitous outcome, as in the conclusion of some tragedies.

CATHARSIS A concept introduced by Aristotle whereby the emotions of pity and fear aroused by a tragedy are 'purged' from the spectator. Catharsis can be thought of as Aristotle's answer to the following problem: since pity and fear are not pleasurable emotions in themselves, how is it that watching a tragedy that arouses pity and fear is a pleasurable experience?

CHORUS In a play, a group of people with a single identity, which may participate in the action in some way and both sings and dances. Essential in ancient Greek tragedy and Old Comedy, and in some other traditions such as Japanese Noh theatre, but rare in Western plays after antiquity. In some later plays the name Chorus is given (somewhat inappropriately) to a single narrator and/or commentator.

CLIMACTIC STRUCTURE A way of structuring plays where the action 'rises' by means of complication to a climax and then 'falls' through a denouement or to a catastrophe. Often equated with 'Freytag's pyramid'.

CLIMAX A major turning point in the action as a whole or in some segment of it.

COMEDY One of the two main polarities of dramatic fiction, the other being tragedy. A non-serious treatment of either serious or non-serious themes, evoking amusement or laughter in the audience and with a plot that ends happily. There are many different kinds, or sub-genres, of comedy.

COMEDY OF MANNERS A form of comedy in which humour is derived from the social values and social behaviour of a particular contemporary social group, often the upper classes. Comedy of manners is typically 'high comedy' with wit and plot complication playing much greater parts than physical or visual humour. Its aim is often to satirize contemporary mores.

COMEDY OF VICE AND FOLLY A form of comedy in which foolish characters are duped and preyed on by vicious ones. In the end, the former suffer only public exposure but the latter are punished, usually by the legal authority.

COMMEDIA DELL'ARTE A general term for a style of theatre performed throughout Europe, mainly by Italian troupes, between around 1550 and 1750. In Commedia dell'Arte, plays were improvised, not scripted, based on a given scenario and involving stock characters of three main types: 1) serious characters, especially young lovers; 2) semi-serious characters, commonly old men or masters with peculiar characteristics; and 3) the true comic characters (such as Arlecchino), mostly servants, collectively called *Zanni*, who were not only involved in the plot but could also undertake independent clowning routines or *lazzi*. Although not a literary tradition, the Commedia style had enormous influence on comic dramatists, especially Goldoni and Moliere, and more recently Fo. More generally, many common character types in later scripted comedy are found in Commedia.

COMPLICATION An incident in the plot which delays the resolution. More generally, the second phase of the plot comprising various such incidents.

CONFLICT A situation that arises either externally because different characters have incompatible goals, or internally because an individual character has different incompatible goals. Conflict is commonly held to be essential to drama, at least in the western tradition.

CONVENTION A generally approved way of doing something. A shared understanding between playwright, director and actors on the one hand and the audience on the other that a specific means of presenting something on stage is acceptable.

CROSS CASTING Casting against character, usually when women play men and/or men play women.

CURTAIN A rise in the action that generates suspense or creates a climax immediately before the fall of the curtain at the end of an act.

DENOUEMENT An unraveling of the complications of the plot which immediately precedes the conclusion of the play.

DESIGNER One who collaborates creatively with the director in preparing a production of a play by developing and refining its visual presentation, whether this be its set, or costumes, or lighting.

DEUS EX MACHINA Latin phrase (a translation of the original Greek *apo mechane theos*) meaning 'the god from the machine.' In ancient Greek theatre, a crane was sometimes used to introduce a god into the play from above, as if from the sky, usually at the end of a play and in order to resolve otherwise intractable problems. By extension, any device that achieves resolution of the plot in an arbitrary and contrived way.

DIALOGUE The spoken words of a play, where this involves alternation of different speaking voices.

DIRECT ADDRESS Where an actor speaks directly to the audience, either in character or out of character.

DIRECTOR Person responsible for the specific interpretation of a play in production and for the artistic integration of the different elements of production.

DOMESTIC DRAMA Drama set in rooms in private houses and dealing with the lives of middle or lower class characters.

DOWNSTAGE The part of the playing space closest to the audience.

DOUBLING The use of one actor to play more than one part in the play.

DRAMATIST A writer of plays. A playwright.

DRAMATURGY The general principles of dramatic art.

DUMB SHOW Traditionally, a pantomime presenting some part of the action of a play before that action is played in full with speeches.

ENTRANCE The entry of an actor into the playing space representing the arrival of a character within the fictional setting of the scene. Also a part of the playing space or set where this occurs.

EPIC THEATRE A politicized version of the concept of episodic structure. An idea developed and elaborated by Bertolt Brecht of what he believed to be the most desirable structure of plays where the playwright's intention is to promote a critical attitude in the spectators towards the society which is represented. In epic theatre, plays consist of relatively many short scenes each of which is relatively self-contained and has its own dramatic and perhaps pedagogical point. Breaks between the scenes allow spectators to think critically about what has just been seen, rather than being swept along by a continuous action. Because of the frequency of scene changes, epic plays can cover a great amount of time and space – hence the name 'epic,' since this is true of epic poems too. Brecht contrasted epic theatre to what he called 'dramatic theatre' or 'Aristotelian theatre,' both of which terms refer to what is more commonly called climactic structure.

EPISODE In ancient Greek tragedy, a scene involving the characters in which the plot is advanced. An episode is followed by a *stasimon* in which the chorus dances and sings. More generally, a set of closely connected events which constitutes a particular phase or segment of a plot.

EPISODIC STRUCTURE A way of structuring plays where the action is divided into a number of more or less self-contained episodes which are relatively loosely connected in a sequence.

EXIT The departure of an actor from the playing space representing the departure of a character from the fictional setting of the scene.

EXPOSITION The first part of a play which establishes the situation and introduces the central characters.

FADE OUT Gradual, smooth transition from a lit stage to an unlit one.

FARCE A form of comedy characterized by a high degree of complication of the plot, rapid pace of action and plot development, simplified characters and often a high proportion of slapstick-type visual gags. Sometimes, farcical episodes or incidents occur in comedies of other kinds.

FICTIONAL TIME The time which is presumed to pass during some part of the story, or which would need to pass if the action were real.

FREEZE A technique or device in which the actors onstage hold their positions without moving.

FREYTAG'S PYRAMID The 'shape' of a climactic plot in which the action 'rises' to a climax then 'falls' to a resolution.

FOURTH WALL An imaginary plane which separates the staged action from the audience as if it were a wall. In fourth wall dramas, the actors act as if they are unaware of the presence of an audience. The fourth wall is essential in naturalistic drama.

GREATER DIONYSIA The Spring festival in ancient Athens in honour of the god Dionysos during which tragedies were performed over a period of three days and comedies were performed on a fourth day. From about 530 BCE a prize was given for the best tragedy and from 486 BCE a prize was given for the best comedy. Also called the City Dionysia.

HAMARTIA A tragic flaw in or an error of judgment by the tragic hero that leads ultimately to a change from happiness to misery.

HIGH COMEDY A form of comedy in which humour is intellectual and refined, typically witty, and mainly derived from the lifestyles, values and manners of the well-born. Closely related to comedy of manners.

HISTORY PLAY A play which dramatizes events of historical significance.

HISTRIONIC Adjective describing a kind or style of acting characterized by grand gestures and declamatory speech.

ITALIAN STAGE A playing space with the audience on one side only and framed by a proscenium arch. Also called a picture frame stage.

LIGHTING PLOT The sequence of lighting changes through a performance. Some of these changes may be written explicitly into the play text.

LINES What actors speak, have to learn and occasionally forget.

LOW COMEDY A form of comedy in which humour is usually vulgar or physical, often derived from the lifestyles and behaviour of the low-born.

MELODRAMA Originally a kind of popular nineteenth-century play with relatively simple characters and a plot enacting a confrontation between good and evil, with parts of the action accompanied by music. Nowadays the term is used to signify drama that lacks subtlety.

MESSENGER A character who brings news of some offstage action or event. Sometimes a messenger is no more than a messenger, but at other times s/he has some other role in the plot as well.

METHOD ACTING An approach to acting developed by Lee Strasberg, Stella Adler and Stanford Meisner, based on Stanislavski's system. Method acting aims at communicating the psychological depth of characters. The actor must build the character *from within* rather than by external indications. As far as possible the actor must actually experience the emotions and impulses of the character rather than simply pretending to.

MIME The representation by means of appropriate physical movement (and without use of speech) of actions involving either objects or settings usually without using anything else to represent these objects or settings. Also called pantomime.

MIMESIS Imitation or representation. The associated adjective is *mimetic*. (The Greek root of the word 'mime'.)

MONOLOGUE A relatively long, uninterrupted speech by a single character.

MORALITY PLAY A type of medieval Christian play enacting allegories of vice and virtue. Morality plays were didactic in purpose but often included entertaining comic scenes.

MYSTERY PLAY A type of medieval Christian play enacting Bible stories. Like morality plays, mystery plays came to include comic scenes for entertainment.

NATURALISM A style of drama that emerged in the late nineteenth century and that aimed at strict verisimilitude in the representation of contemporary life. In naturalistic theatre, characters speak in ordinary, everyday language and do not make soliloquies or asides. Sets are 'full' and include more objects than necessary for the action. The fourth wall is strictly observed. Naturalistic plays are commonly set in rooms and are a kind of domestic drama but they commonly deal with social issues and problems.

NATYASASTRA An important Sanskrit treatise or 'Drama Manual' on the arts of Indian theatre and acting written between 200 BCE and 300 CE.

NEW COMEDY The comedy of Menander and more generally of the fourth century BCE in Athens, and of Plautus and Terence in Rome. New Comedy focused on domestic life, whereas Old Comedy had focused on public life. It developed a range of stock characters and its intricate plots had significant influence on the development of comedy in Renaissance Europe.

NOH THEATRE Traditional, highly stylized from of Japanese theatre dating from the fourteenth century which tells usually simple stories by means of spoken and sung dialogue, dance, music and a chorus. The most famous author of Noh plays and of treatises on the art of acting and playwriting is Zeami (1363-1443).

OBJECTIVE In Stanislavski's system of acting, what a character wants to achieve at some particular point of the play.

OFFSTAGE An adjective referring literally to the wings and backstage area of the theatre but used also to define an extension of the fictional setting where actions and events in the story which are not enacted onstage are presumed to take place.

OLD COMEDY The comedy of the mid to late fifth century BCE in Athens, especially the plays of Aristophanes (since these are the only examples that survive). Old Comedy was both more anarchic in its comic impulse and more satirical in its intention, and made much greater use of the chorus, than the New Comedy that replaced it.

ONSTAGE An adjective referring to the playing space as seen by the audience.

ORCHESTRA The circular playing space – literally a 'dancing space' – of an ancient Greek theatre. The space occupied by the chorus in an ancient Greek play, but open to the actors/characters as well.

OVER-PLAYING Exaggerated and untruthful acting.

PANTOMIME Originally a kind of Roman dance-drama. Nowadays either a) a simple synonym for mime or b) a type of traditional play performed in Britain around Christmas time, based on a fairy tale, with cross casting (the 'Principal Boy' being played by a young woman and the 'Pantomime Dames' by male comedians), comedy, songs and audience participation.

PERIPETEIA A reversal of fortune.

PICTURE FRAME STAGE A playing space with the audience on one side and framed by a proscenium arch. Also called an Italian stage.

PLAYWRIGHT A maker or author of plays. A dramatist.

PLOT A sequence of events that constitutes a story. In plays, the sequence of events that are enacted on stage.

POETICS An important and influential work by Aristotle composed around 330 BCE which discusses the nature of tragedy.

POOR THEATRE A style of theatre that uses little in the way of sets, props, costume and technical resources but relies on the energy and inventiveness of actors to stimulate the imagination of the audience. Similar to rough theatre, although Jerzy Grotowski used the term to signify an almost 'monastic' approach to theatre with a spiritual goal.

PROBLEM PLAY A play that cannot be easily be classified as to type or genre, usually because it mixes elements of different types or genres. Sometimes this term is used quite differently to mean a play which presents a social problem together with different points of view about it.

PRODUCTION A particular theatrical interpretation or staging of a play. There can be different productions of the same play and different performances of the same production.

PROLOGUE The opening scene of some plays that either introduces the play or very obviously serves the purpose of exposition.

PROMENADE THEATRE A type or style of theatrical production in which the action moves from place to place, either outdoors or indoors, so that the audience must walk to follow it.

PROP Short for 'stage property'. An object used by an actor to advance the action in some way, but which is not part of the set.

PROSCENIUM ARCH An arch that frames the playing area as seen by the audience.

PROTAGONIST Literally, the 'first competitor'. Nowadays, the central character in the play, the one whose actions principally drive the plot.

RECOGNITION A change from ignorance to knowledge on the part of a character which is often an important turning point in the plot. Sometimes the Greek *anagnorisis* is used.

RESOLUTION The part of the plot that follows its climax and in which certain problems are solved.

RESTORATION COMEDY A witty, urbane, cynical and sexually explicit style of English comedy that flourished from the mid 1660s to about 1700, though tending gradually to become more morally conventional from the mid 1680s. Restoration comedy satirizes many of the pretensions and hypocrisy of the upper classes, but often seems to endorse the amoral outlook and self-gratifying behaviour of the witty rake-hero.

REVERSAL A change of fortune or situation, from good to bad or from bad to good. Sometimes the Greek *peripeteia* is used.

ROLE A part in a play. A character in a drama as seen by an actor.

ROMANTIC COMEDY A form of comedy in which humour is mainly derived from the complications, often including mistaken identities, that prevent lovers being together or marrying. The plot of Romantic Comedy proceeds towards the resolution of all difficulties and typically ends with marriage or the promise of marriage.

ROUGH THEATRE A style of theatre that uses little in the way of sets, props, costume and technical resources but relies on the energy and inventiveness of actors to stimulate the imagination of the audience. Similar to poor theatre, although Peter Brook used the term to distinguish it from Grotowski's more spiritually oriented sense of poor theatre.

SATIRE A particular use of comedy or of comic devices, especially exaggeration, intended to draw attention to aspects of contemporary society as in need of change.

SCENE A self-contained segment of the plot, a sequence of connected events or actions that occur continuously without any jump in time or place.

SCRIPT The written text of a play.

SET The onstage representation of the setting of the onstage action. The set is real while the setting is fictional.

SKENE The stage building at the back of the *orchestra* in ancient Greek theatre that was used to represent part of the setting such as a palace or temple or cave.

SOLILOQUY A type of monologue in which a character is alone onstage and thinks aloud. Soliloquies privilege the audience as a kind of 'eavesdropper' rather than being directly addressed to the audience.

STAGE DIRECTION A part of a play text that specifies the setting or set, or an action, or how a speech sounds.

STAGE LEFT The left of the playing space as seen by a performer looking towards the audience.

STAGE RIGHT The right of the playing space as seen by a performer looking towards the audience.

STAGE TIME The time it takes to enact something onstage.

STASIMON (Plural *stasima*) A section of an ancient Greek tragedy, between two episodes, in which the chorus sings and dances.

STORY-TELLER An actor or character in a play who narrates some part of the story directly to the audience.

STUDIO THEATRE A small-scale, intimate and flexible theatre space.

SUB-PLOT In some plays, a secondary plot or sequence of connected events usually involving a main character who is either a secondary character in the main plot or not directly involved in it. One of the main functions of a sub-plot is to provide contrasts with the main plot.

SUBTEXT What a character *means* where this is not exactly the same as what s/he *says*.

SUPER-OBJECTIVE In Stanislavski's system of acting, what a character wants to achieve in the play as a whole.

TABLEAU A stage picture which is meaningful as an image and in which the characters are temporarily still, perhaps in a freeze.

THEATRE IN THE ROUND A playing space with the audience on four sides or arranged in a circle around it. The same as an arena stage.

THESIS PLAY A play that is constructed so that it serves to demonstrate or prove a point (the thesis), usually a criticism of contemporary society.

THESPIAN Another name for an actor derived from the name Thespis. According to legend, Thespis was the first tragedian in ancient Greece and the first man to step out from the chorus in order to engage in dialogue with it.

THRUST STAGE A playing space with the audience on three sides. The same as an apron stage.

TRAGEDIAN A writer of tragedies.

TRAGEDY One of the two main polarities of dramatic fiction, the other being comedy. A type of serious play involving a change from happiness to misery for one or more characters usually as a result of an error of judgment or an excessive passion on the part of one of these characters and which arouses pity and fear in the audience.

TRAGIC FLAW A weakness of character or an error of judgment by the tragic hero that leads ultimately to a change from happiness to misery. Sometimes the Greek *hamartia* is used.

TRAGICOMEDY A kind of play where it seems equally appropriate to laugh at events and characters as to be disturbed by those events and to pity the characters.

TRILOGY A group of three plays in sequence with a single connected plot.

UNDER-PLAYING A style of acting which aims to focus only on the most significant aspects of speech and action by avoiding all 'unnecessary' characterization and any exaggeration of tone and gesture.

UNITIES In the plural, the so-called three unities: firstly, the unity of time, which requires that the action take place within one day; secondly, the unity of place, which requires that the action take place in a single location; thirdly, the unity of action, which requires that nothing irrelevant to the plot is included in the play.

UPSTAGE The part of the playing space furthest away from the audience.

WINGS Offstage areas to the left and right of the playing space.

ZANNI Generic name for comic servants in Commedia dell'Arte, characters who often had a 'life of their own' beyond the specific story-line of the play being performed.

Index of Playwrights and Plays

AESCHYLUS 94, 103
Agamemnon (458 BCE) 27, 44, 82, 86, 105
ALBEE, EDWARD
Who's Afraid of Virginia Woolf (1962) 31
ANOUILH, JEAN 105
Antigone (1944) 94, 95, 106, 111
ARISTOPHANES 109
Lysistrata (411 BCE) 109-10
ARISTOTLE
Poetics (*ca.* 330 BCE) 11, 15, 33, 54, 56, 58-60, 61, 63, 95, 97, 101-2, 105, 107
AYCKBOURN, ALAN 96
BECKETT, SAMUEL 33, 92, 111
Act Without Words I (1956) 13
Act Without Words II (1956) 13
Waiting for Godot (1953) 26, 27, 32, 43, 53, 64, 66, 97, 111
BOAL, AUGUSTO 98-9
BOND, EDWARD 55
BRECHT, BERTOLT 28, 58, 79-81, 97-8, 104
The Caucasian Chalk Circle (1944-5) 85
Mother Courage and her Children (1941) 20, 37, 80-1, 98, 105
CHEKHOV, ANTON 32-3, 46, 66, 75, 76
The Cherry Orchard (1903) 14, 32-33, 46, 75, 76, 110, 111
The Seagull (1898) 32, 75, 76, 110
The Three Sisters (1901) 32, 46, 75, 76
Uncle Vanya (1899) 32
CHURCHILL, CARYL
Cloud Nine (1979) 82-3, 86
Heart's Desire (from Blue Heart) (1997) 65, 66, 68
Top Girls (1982) 68
Vinegar Tom (1976) 36, 38, 81
EURIPIDES 58, 95, 103
The Bacchae (405 BCE) 86
Medea (431 BCE) 94, 105
FO, DARIO
Accidental Death of an Anarchist (1970) 47-8, 49, 106
FRIEL, BRIAN 96
FUGARD, ATHOL
The Island (1973) 16-7, 83
Sizwe Bansi is Dead (1972) 83
Statements After an Arrest Under the Immorality Act (1972) 77-8, 86
GOLDONI, CARLO 49
HARE, DAVID
Fanshen (1975) 98
Stuff Happens (2004) 85
HAVEL, VACLAV
The Increased Difficulty of Concentration (1968) 68

Protest (1978) 42, 44
IBSEN, HENRIK 13, 25, 75
A Doll's House (1879) 48, 77, 94
Ghosts (1881) 23, 26, 53, 55, 56, 57, 62
Hedda Gabler (1890) 25, 27, 29, 38, 39-40, 43, 55-6, 75, 76, 77
Little Eyolf (1894) 75
The Master Builder (1892) 75
The Pillars of the Community (1877) 75
IONESCO, EUGENE
The Bald Soprano (1950) 56, 66, 67
JONSON, BEN 56, 96-7
Volpone (1606) 87, 90, 106, 107
KALIDASA
The Recognition of Sakuntala (between 200 BCE and 400 CE) 33, 36, 72-3, 83
KYD, THOMAS 103
The Spanish Tragedy (1584-94) 103
LORCA, FREDERICO GARCIA
Blood Wedding (1933) 36, 105, 106
The House of Bernarda Alba (1936) 25, 31
MAMET, DAVID 96
MARLOWE, CHRISTOPHER
The Tragical History of Doctor Faustus (*ca.* 1592) 62, 63-4, 67, 104
MENANDER 109
MILLER, ARTHUR
Death of a Salesman (1949) 67, 75, 105
MISHIMA, YUKIO
Five Modern Noh Plays (1950-55) 94, 95
MOLIERE, JEAN BAPTISTE 49
Tartuffe (1667) 25, 37, 66, 107
NORTON, THOMAS and THOMAS SACKVILLE
Gorboduc (1561) 103
O'NEILL, EUGENE 14
Long Day's Journey Into Night (1956) 14, 45
Mourning Becomes Electra (1931) 94
PINTER, HAROLD 43, 46, 92, 96
Betrayal (1979) 68
The Caretaker (1960) 43
Old Times (1971) 14, 44, 46, 92, 96
PLAUTUS 109
RACINE, JEAN
Phèdre (1677) 59
ROZEWICZ, TADEUSZ
The Card Index (1960) 68-9, 97
SENECA 13, 103
SHAFFER, PETER 96
Equus (1973) 86
SHAKESPEARE, WILLIAM 52, 56-7, 59, 82, 83, 92, 95-6, 103
(Most dates given below are uncertain.)
Hamlet (1600-01) 10, 15, 36, 38, 41, 44, 51, 60-2, 67, 71, 87, 110
Henry V (1598-99) 73, 83
King Lear (1605-06) 30-1, 74, 79
Macbeth (1605-06) 40, 43, 84, 103
A Midsummer Night's Dream (1594-96) 87, 110
Measure for Measure (1604-05) 37, 52, 66, 110
Othello (1603-04) 94, 103
Richard III (1592-93) 40
The Taming of the Shrew (1593-94) 66
The Tempest (1611-12) 31, 83
Twelfth Night (1599-1600) 52, 62-3, 87

The Winter's Tale (1610-11) 31-2, 67, 87
SHERIDAN, RICHARD
The School for Scandal (1777) 109
SOPHOCLES 58, 95, 103
Antigone (445-42 BCE) 17, 29
Oedipus the King (*ca.* 430 BCE) 22-3, 27, 54, 57, 59, 64, 93-4
SOYINKA, WOLE
The Bacchae of Euripides: a Communion Rite (1973) 83, 86-7, 94, 95
STANISLAVSKI, KONSTANTIN 38, 43, 71, 75, 76, 110
STOPPARD, TOM 96
STRINDBERG, AUGUST 25, 33, 75, 104
The Dance of Death (1900) 75
The Father (1888) 31, 48, 75
Miss Julie (1889) 75, 104
TERENCE 109
WEBSTER, JOHN
The Duchess of Malfi (1613) 41-2, 74, 79, 104
WYCHERLEY, WILLIAM
The Country Wife (*ca.* 1674) 108, 109
WILDE, OSCAR
The Importance of Being Earnest (1895) 56, 57, 66, 107
Salome (1894, 1892 in French) 73-4
ZEAMI 55

Books for the IB from Anagnosis

Theory of Knowledge

The Enterprise of Knowledge 2nd ed.
by **John L. Tomkinson**

The original and most comprehensive ToK text now thoroughly revised and updated
- comprehensive IB curriculum coverage
- clear explanations of logical concepts
- challenging and up-to-date examples
- detailed illustrative case studies
- ideas for class discussion
- ideas for student presentations
- index of concepts

History

Studies in Twentieth Century World History
Wars and Warfare
Single-Party States
The Cold War

- clear explanations of essential concepts
- number system for instant reference
- accessible to students lacking background
- thought- provoking analyses
- subject-specific help in essay-writing
- format designed for examination revision

Chemistry

Chemistry Experiments by Marketos & Rouvas
A laboratory manual designed for IB Chemistry

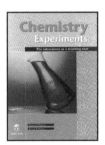

The experiments are designed to:
- develop the ability to record data
- analyse data
- comment critically upon procedures
- teach experimental techniques
- link experimental work and theory
- assist understanding of basic concepts

All Anagnosis books can be ordered online by credit card from:
www.anagnosis.gr

For up-to-date information about Anagnosis books:
visit our website: **www.anagnosis.gr**
email: info@anagnosis.gr

Anagnosis, Deliyianni 3, Maroussi, 15122 Athens, Greece
telephone: ++30-210-62-54-654
fax: ++30-210-62-54-089